D1561778

The Causes of Human Behavior

The Causes of
Human Behavior

Implications for Theory and
Method in the Social Sciences

Lawrence B. Mohr

Ann Arbor

THE UNIVERSITY OF MICHIGAN PRESS

Copyright © by the University of Michigan 1996
All rights reserved
Published in the United States of America by
The University of Michigan Press
Manufactured in the United States of America
⊗ Printed on acid-free paper

1999   1998   1997   1996   4   3   2   1

A CIP catalog record for this book is available from the British Library.

Library of Congress Cataloging-in-Publication Data

Mohr, Lawrence B.
    The causes of human behavior : implications for theory and method
in the social sciences / Lawrence B. Mohr.
        p.   cm.
    Includes bibliographical references and index.
    ISBN 0-472-10665-1 (hardcover : alk. paper)
    1. Psychology.   2. Human behavior.   I. Title.
BF121.M5794   1996
300′.1—dc20   95-52492
                                                                   CIP

Contents

Preface

Several related premises addressing problems in modern explanatory social science underlie this work. The disciplines are supposed to be cumulative, but there is little in the way of accumulated, general theory. Much scholarly work strives toward generalizations, but true, broadly applicable laws have proven elusive. At the same time, the more qualitative approaches to the explanation of behavior have seemed limited in their applicability and general usefulness. Such apparent problems need to be viewed both realistically and rigorously; a dialogue about the appropriate means and ends of social research, based in an analysis of the fundamental issues, has long been warranted.

In prior empirical work, much of it centered around explaining innovation in organizations, I had arrived at the conclusions (*a*) that people's motives or reasons for undertaking certain behaviors could not form part of general laws governing those behaviors, but (*b*) that these same motives or reasons could, in the individual case, cause the behaviors to be carried out. Both of these conclusions seemed at the time, and still do in fact, seem sensible and reasonable, and perhaps even true. The more I thought about them, however, the more contradictory and generally puzzling they became, and the more I realized that much in both of them was essentially vague. The present treatise grew out of the attempt to clear up the dozen or so issues of puzzlement and vagueness resident in those positions so that I might evaluate them properly. From the very beginning, I was asking questions *about* explanatory research rather than doing it, and as I continued, this departure became ever more pronounced. I felt, however, that it would be somehow worthwhile to push on, and the present volume is the result.

Whether my intuition about worthwhileness was correct is for readers and critics to judge, but I can take the opportunity of this preface to report, at any rate, what appeared to me to result. My approach was to single out for special attention two of the issues that seemed primary—causation and the behavior-generating mechanism—hoping that these would give me some purchase on the others. After a few years, with some disappointment, I felt that I was working on a number of intriguing but fairly independent questions. Still another year into the project, however, I perceived quite suddenly, and with surprise, that the pieces did indeed fall together. For me, at least, they had developed to form an interlocking whole—one that promised to address a broad range of methodological issues with definiteness and that essentially forced a kind of worldview of the place of social research in science and society. Merit aside, the outcome still seems to me serendipitous.

As a whole, the project has been the most enjoyable of my professional career, but it came with a sense of dismay and frustration over one dilemma. Rightly or wrongly, I felt that I could not get the help I needed in addressing my questions without detouring sharply into other disciplines, particularly philosophy and physiological psychology. I was essentially an amateur in both but, with some relish, set about trying to learn as much as I could in the areas that seemed critical. When I began the writing itself, I felt I had no choice but to impart what seemed to be the important lessons from these other disciplines, interwoven with those from my own fields of social research. Trial reactions to the initial outcomes, however, reinforced beyond a shadow of a doubt what had begun to become apparent during the process itself, namely, that these are not simply different disciplines, but different cultures. What I wrote held almost no interest for natives of the other tribes because I spoke to *their* issues without showing an appreciation of a large proportion of the *connections* that, in their culture, are essential for the treatment of those issues. At the same time, the more of these connections I tried to include in order to strengthen my use of the materials—and I never did become acculturated enough to be thoroughly successful at this—the more I left the members of my own tribe dazed, bored, negative, and often resentful. The problem was compounded by the shared nature of much of the subject matter; all three of these cultures deal extensively with the issue of the determinants of human behavior, but from different and, as I became increasingly aware, mutually unintelligible perspectives—especially between philosophy and empirical social research. I could not find a totally successful middle ground. I tend to think that there is none and can be none, but I would welcome an exemplar more adroit than my own.

In attempting to resolve the dilemma, my intended primary audience was clear—practicing empirical social researchers, whether of the quantitative or qualitative stripe, and especially those with at least a passing interest in methodological self-examination. I came to give up all intention of appealing to the interests of philosophers, political theorists, or brain scientists. In the end I therefore included as little of the borrowings from these other disciplines as I could while still showing some inescapable grounding for my essential arguments and conclusions, but I fear that what is left will still be a liability for the treatise in the eyes of some of my intended audience. This aspect of the experience has been almost purely a source of difficulty, but there is perhaps one potentially constructive residue, and that is an empirical research interest for the future in the crossing of cultural boundaries.

Many friends and colleagues have taken the trouble to read parts of this manuscript in its various incarnations and their criticisms and advice have been invaluable. This was particularly true when I was dipping into fields whose culture was strange to me. I am especially grateful for the time and trouble taken by Eugene Bardach, Bill Broder, Douglas Dion, Daniela Gobetti, Richard Hall, George Julnes, Louis Loeb, and Jack Meiland. Valuable directions also arose out of conversations on the developing ideas with Paul Boghossian, Nancy Burns, Michael Lewis-Beck, Daniel Lucich, Mortimer Mishkin, Rick Mohr, Kim Scheppele, and David Velleman. I am grateful to my wife, Elizabeth Hawthorne, for maintaining the faith. And lastly, I want to express a special debt of gratitude to Colin Day and Malcolm Litchfield of the University of Michigan Press, in part for their comments and criticisms on portions of the written text, but especially for standing with me throughout the long and arduous process of shaping an awkward manuscript into an acceptable book.

Introduction

In this book, I take up several fundamental issues in the methodology of explanatory social research from the research practitioner's point of view. The suggestion of my study is that such methodological issues have a bearing on the means and ends of common research practice. Before sketching the plan of the book, I will briefly establish most of the major questions to be treated and characterize the answers I will offer. In this introduction, the questions and answers are organized into three brief sections following the present one, which elaborates the basic issues from which the questions and answers are derived.

As background, let us consider such questions as (*a*) whether the design of explanatory social research must be comparative in order to generate legitimate causal inferences and valid generalizations, (*b*) whether we can have universal laws of human behavior, and (*c*) whether there are fundamental methodological differences between the disciplines of history and, say, political science. A special word is in order about laws: few practitioners in the social and behavioral disciplines would claim today that there are universal laws governing human behavior. Moreover, many would consider the question to be trivial and uninteresting. Perhaps there are no such laws, they would hold, but no matter, the issue has no significant bearing on the conduct of inquiry. I suggest, however, that it is not an uninteresting question for the following reason: much of the research that strives toward the discovery and formulation of theoretical generalizations seems to presume that attaining the goal of universal laws or *systematic* generalizations (i.e., those for which any limiting conditions are specified) is possible. Otherwise, it becomes difficult, not impossible, perhaps, but difficult, to say just what the meaning and import of such "theoretical" generalizations might be. How, exactly, shall we specify their value, given that they might lose their force radically with a change in study population or time period? Thus, the issue of laws, universal laws, or systematic generalizations is first a question of whether they are attainable and, if they are not, of exactly how to specify the import of the sorts of generalizations we do generate and would like to consider theoretical.

My thesis is that a good deal of light can be shed on certain important questions by accomplishing two critical tasks. The first is to achieve clarity on the concept of causation, and the second is to understand the physiological mechanism that generates individual, intentional behavior. Achieving clarity on causation is necessary because questions regarding the sorts of comparative or other designs that are valid, or regarding the relative power of designs, are bound up at least in part with the capacity of such designs to demonstrate causation. Also, the issue of universal laws may well be found to concern causal laws, even when the goal is the explanation of human behavior. In order to speak rigorously about such issues as design and laws, I suggest that we avoid unstated or loosely conceived notions of the underlying concept of causation. In fact, we use and rely on the idea of causation ubiquitously in research but usually without being meticulous about its meaning. Further, I will make the case that when the meaning of causation actually is specified, the validity of the definitions offered is problematic.

The second critical task, to understand the physiological mechanism that generates individual, intentional behavior, includes the relation of such a mechanism to the kinds of factors social scientists tend to use to explain behavior. The need for this knowledge arises because of our interest both in the control of behavior and in the possibility of laws or other stable generalizations that might cover it. As to control, common explanations of behavior based on motives, desires, reasons, decisions, choices, and so forth—roughly, what is wanted or intended by individuals and groups—apparently assume that people are in control of their behavior. If they are not—if they do not control their behavior through their reasons, decisions, or choices—then there would seem to be little point in invoking such states and events as parts of theoretical explanations. Control, in turn, would be considered by many to be a physical sort of concept; that is, it may readily be taken to imply such physical intervention as causing or allowing behaviors to happen or preventing them from taking place. Thus, it is well to be aware of the physical mechanism involved in the production of intentional behavior and the relation that reasons, decisions, and the like might have to regulating it. If the physical mechanism, on the one hand, and these mental concepts, on the other, are not well integrated, common social science explanations based on such concepts might well be wrongheaded.

Similarly, an interest in laws strongly recommends a knowledge of the physical underpinnings of behavior because there frequently is a close connection between laws and the physical workings of the world. If our attempts to achieve systematic generalizations are serious, we should be aware of the kinds of generalizations, if any, that might be consistent with viewing behavior and its determinants as physical concepts.

What is the physiological mechanism that generates intentional behavior? What categories of things can be the physical determinants of behavior? What, if anything, do these entities have to do with social science; that is, are physical behavioral acts and their physical causes susceptible to being treated as a natural part of social science or are they a matter only for the physiological disciplines? If the latter, then to what sorts of causal explanation, if any, can the social sciences aspire?

The following questions and answers, which form a brief sketch of the material covered in the remainder of the book, indicate the relations between these two basic tasks and several more specific issues with significant bearing on the practice of social research. For the sake of brevity and as an overview, the questions and answers are presented quite simply at this point. For that reason, certain positions might strike some readers as disconnected, unfounded, or extreme, depending on one's own background and perspective. I hope that the more nuanced treatment of the issues in the chapters that follow will do justice to their true complexity.

The Causes of Intentional Behavior

Perhaps causation, which is certainly relevant in physics, is not so relevant in social science. Is it true, for example, that much human behavior is not amenable to the ordinary pursuit of causal explanation because it tends to be greatly overdetermined—that is, because, in its complexity, human behavior is affected and conditioned by a large number of contributing and alternative factors? This question, which seems to hold out hope of an excuse for avoiding the issue of causation, is itself evasive; it begs itself internally. There is no way to claim that human behavior is "overdetermined" without thereby admitting the relevance of causality. The concept of causality is widely used. The premise here is that it is better to meet it head on than to dismiss it with casual argumentation.

To speak rigorously about such issues as the causes of human behavior, one must give the term *cause* a clear meaning. Causal terminology occurs and reoccurs relentlessly in the descriptions, explanations, conclusions, and inferences of social research, and causality is the criterion that distinguishes between supposedly strong research designs, such as the randomized experiment, and weaker ones, such as quasi experiments, correlational designs, and case studies. What sense of *cause* gives legitimate meaning to these statements and criteria? The interpretations of the term that are relied upon in the social disciplines tend to be based either in (*a*) the regularity theory of causation, which entails that inferring causation in the individual case depends on being able to locate that case as an instance of a general law or (*b*) the counterfactual definition, which roots causation in the knowledge that if X had not occurred, then neither would Y. Can either of these serve as the rigorous basis for causal discourse in social science? If not, is there another conceptualization that can? My response will be to argue that these two cannot serve in the required way. I will briefly emphasize the shortcomings of the regularity theory, or the Humean view, in the social science context and lay out at some length the serious deficiencies of the counterfactual definition. Based on this review, I will offer an alternative, dual conceptualization of causality, one that withstands the challenges raised against the important approaches offered in the past and that I hope will also be found to be congenial to social scientists. In part, the dual view modifies the counterfactual definition in such a way as to overcome its analytical deficiencies while vindicating the utility of its basic thrust.

What, fundamentally, causes intentional behavior? Is it certain thoughts, for example, such as decisions, conscious reasons, or choices? That is, is it true that the conscious choice to be a more democratic supervisor will cause one to supervise more democratically? If today is election day and if a certain man decides that he will vote in the evening and does not change his mind, will that decision cause him to vote? When one grapples with this general issue, one realizes that the following question, although it may appear oversimplified on the surface, can in fact be surprisingly troublesome: is there a relation between the thought and the appropriate behavior that is similar to the relation between the light switch and the light? The question is troublesome because it is awkward to answer either yes or no. If one's tentative answer is yes, then how can we explain all of those times when a person has a conscious reason or makes a definite decision but does not carry out the behavior? That is not like flipping a switch. If, on the other hand, one's tentative answer is no, then we must apparently be prepared to accept that our behavior is not under our own control, so that there is a need to solve the puzzle of just how it really does come about and to wonder whether the answer will be demeaning to humanity. I hope to show that, given common and, I think, correct assumptions about the ways in which causality operates in the world, thoughts are never causes. They may correlate fairly well with behavior and may frequently be significant inputs into the causal system, but they do not determine that a behavior will take place, nor what it will be if it does take place.

In a paper that is still widely read by social scientists and that is at the heart of the positivist approach, Hempel (1942) suggested that people do certain things in certain situations because those are the rational things to do. In other words, people generally, or at least frequently, do things for reasons. Although it is not always obvious, this thrust is at the bottom of a great deal of theorizing and explanation in the social disciplines (I will elaborate on this claim in chapter 4). Is it then the case that the reasons for which we act are the causes of those actions? This question has received a great deal of attention in philosophy, and I will deal with it briefly in chapter 3. Unfortunately, the arguments on both sides are strong. In the end, I will conclude that, although thoughts do not cause intentional behavior and reasons cannot be causes either to the extent that they are thoughts, still, there is a strong and important sense in which reasons are indeed the causes of intentional human behavior. Clearly, this conclusion depends on the possibility that reasons may exist on some level other than the conscious one. We will see that they do—in a common everyday sense—although the notion is initially puzzling to some. The conclusion that "operative reasons," as we will call them, are the causes of intentional behavior has important consequences for research design and causal explanation.

Can we then rely upon the tenet that human behavior is rational? Apparently not, even though reasons are causes, because if we attribute specific goals to individuals we may very well find that their behavior is not meant to maximize achievement of those goals. Therefore the behavior is not rational in the framework offered. If instead of attributing specific goals to individuals we allow for the full and actual multi-plicity, obscurity, mutability, and subtlety of goals, may we count on rational behavior in pursuit of these whether we as observers know what they are and how they fit together or not? I will conclude that basically we cannot. Behavior proceeds by another paradigm, and although the rational and what I will call the "affect-object" paradigms would frequently predict the same behavior, they also frequently would not.

The brain must be the locus of control over intentional behavior, and the brain is a physical system subject to physical laws. Reasons, however, would seem to be something different—something not subject to physical laws. If the physical brain governs behavior and if reasons cause behavior as well, what facts or relations might reconcile the two? Do reasons have a physical presence in the brain and cause behavior as such? Reasons (according to some anyway) may frequently have a physical presence in the form of thoughts, but, as I have said, thoughts do not cause behavior. Once the physical elements in the brain that do generate intentional behavior are identified, however, it is clear that particular configurations of them may closely be conceptualized as reasons. Arguably, the physical and the rational as causes are reconciled in this relation.

Does affect have a role in determining behavior? If so, just what is that role? Are affect and intentionality, which are often thought of as "emotion versus reason," related to one another? If so, how? I will marshal evidence which indicates that affect is at the core of the physiological system that generates intentional behavior. Although we may not actually sense it or recognize it as such, affect is an integral part of every reason for doing something. More than that, it is the element that makes one reason causal while another coexisting one fails to exert any influence.

Should explanation properly be at the individual level or at the structural or institutional level? My answer here is that all of the intentional behavior we wish to explain in the social disciplines is reducible to individual behavior, which is governed by reasons. Although important and I think instructive, however, this fact has little to do with selecting the best level at which to operate in a given subfield or research project—individual, institutional, and so forth. Powerful causal explanations of aggregate-level as well as individual-level events and characteristics are apparently available, and the issue of what level of research should be carried out is by no means decided on the basis of the definition of causation or the roots of the generation of individual behavior. Similarly, the capability of being reduced to the individual level has little to do with selecting the best match in terms of levels of cause and effect—structural explanations for individual behavior, individual explanations for group behavior, and so on. We will see in chapters 4 through 6 that the findings sketched out here suggest some definite changes in the means and ends of explanatory social research, but they neither support nor undermine the value of any major type or level of research that I know of, with the important exception of research designed to discover general laws. The value of research at any level of aggregation is determined by other criteria, which I will discuss in chapter 5.

The Possibility of Universal Laws

Lurking beneath the surface of a large proportion of the salient methodological issues in social research is the question of the possible generality of findings. Can we, by whatever method, discover systematic explanatory relations in the mainstream of our disciplines? If so, does this mean that our work must properly be comparative, as laws generally are (e.g., "If X then Y, and if not X then not Y"; or, similarly, "The greater the X, the greater the Y.")? If not, do quantitative techniques have an important role to play nevertheless?

To respond, I find that social scientists do have views on the subject of the possibility of explanatory laws of human behavior, but I am not aware that a definitive case has been made either way—either the discovery of a few laws that are accepted within their disciplines as being universally valid, so that the possibility is clearly demonstrated, or a deductive demonstration on the other side that such laws are not possible. I will propose a demonstration of the impossibility of laws or systematic generalizations explaining human behaviors. To accept the demonstration as sound, the reader must share certain assumptions, but they are weak ones; that is, I think that they will be readily accepted.

Let us accept the commonly held view that a true cause once is a true cause always, given the same relevant circumstances. In that case, some of the conclusions characterized above would seem to contradict others. In particular, if reasons or other social science concepts are causes, can it be true nevertheless that there are no causal social science laws? I will suggest that there is no contradiction. We can be confident that, in spite of the fact that there is no possibility of causal laws that govern human behavior, we may establish true causal relations in social research between behaviors and their explanations. The apparent contradiction is clarified in part by the reminder that, for any law, it must be possible in principle to specify the circumstances under which it holds. For human behavior—but also for certain events pertinent to the physical and biological sciences—this requirement is impossible to fulfill, that is, it is inherently impossible to specify the circumstances under which a particular behavior will always be determined by a given set of variables or factors. Events of this type will be labeled "probabilistic encounters," a concept that will be introduced in chapter 1 and elaborated throughout the chapters that follow. For the reason given, probabilistic encounters cannot be covered by laws, but once they have occurred, it is clear that a causal explanation is readily available. Thus, we can have causal relations without causal laws.

It might be countered that the difficulty with the possibility of laws lies only in the insistence on universality. Even if there are no universal laws in social science, there may perhaps be probabilistic ones. I will urge that this is a misconception. It is true that much human behavior is probabilistic—in fact, it is fundamentally so—and also that there are reasonable candidates for probabilistic laws in other sciences. However, the probabilistic component of any generalization in the area of intentional behavior inherently lacks the stability necessary for the statement to be categorized as a law. With this argument added to those on universal laws, I will urge that social scientists view their areas as ones that include no laws of any sort and that we accept this premise fully in considering and specifying the value of social research.

Given that there are no general laws of human behavior, are there fundamental methodological differences between historical research and research in disciplines such as psychology, sociology, and political science? Obviously, there are major differences in the ways in which scholars in these disciplines design their work, but, at bottom, my answer is no. The positivist might say, as many have, that it is the business of the historian or anthropologist to explain specific instances of group or individual behavior, that these explanations, to be valid, must inevitably rest on laws and that it is the business of the economist, sociologist, political scientist, and psychologist to discover those laws. This distinction, however, evaporates with the eschewing of laws. Historians clearly do not use large-n, quantitative designs as frequently as their colleagues in these other disciplines, but I do not see that as a fundamental difference. Rather, I will argue that both the goals of research and the epistemological bases of explanation are identical across these fields. For that reason, I will refer to all of the fields collectively in this book as "social science."

The Research Bases of Causation and Generalization

Can causality be established through large-n, comparative research designs? Yes, but in a limited sense. The kind of causation that can be established in this way will be called "factual causality."

Can the causation of behavior be established through what I will characterize as "nonquantitative" research (that is, research designs that do not feature the comparison between what happens when X does and does not occur, or when X is higher as opposed to lower)? I hope to show, by putting together several of the above strands of inquiry, that the answer is yes, in a basic sense of causation to be called "physical causality." Thus, I will claim that the pure case study can be a firm basis for establishing causal relations in social research, where by "case study" I mean in part a design that contains no contrast of the actual, or observed, sequence with the empirically estimated counterfactual sequence ("If not X, then not Y").

Small-n research, that is, research based on samples of two or even five or six units studied in intensive detail, has had difficulty finding a niche for itself in the methodology of the social disciplines. If causality of some legitimate sort can be established through large-n comparative or "quantitative" designs and also through a case study, can it be established through a small-n study as well? In principle, no. The small-n study is neither fish nor fowl, nor is it a design in its own right. It suffers serious shortcomings when proceeding methodologically by the large-n paradigm and can easily tend to muddy the causal waters when taking the ordinary case study route. Moreover, little or nothing can be gained by trying to manipulate the logic of the small-n design so that the causal reasoning pertinent to large-n research and to the case study supplement one another. I do not suggest that small-n studies have little value. The tendency has been strong, however, to view small-n studies as quantitative designs with special problems. I will suggest that the greatest value will result from abandoning this tack and treating small-sample research totally within the methodological paradigm of the case study, slightly extended.

Can there be valid generalization from the large-n, comparative research design? I will argue that this design can be critical for establishing certain kinds of important fact or description but that it is less important than commonly credited for serving as a basis for theoretical generalization, that is, generalization beyond the subjects and time period observed or the population randomly sampled. Generalization in the true thrust of the term—with the reminder that we nevertheless speak of generalization that is not systematic—is based on other considerations entirely. I will urge that, eschewing laws, we focus on the "creative-selective" generalization of findings that research has shown to be "significant possibilities" in the explanation of behavior. Some may find this end point demoralizing in its modesty. Others will see it as a truly human fulfillment of the challenge posed by the human sciences.

Given this modified view of theoretical generalization, can there be valid generalization from a case study? I will support the view that, unlike some of the "hard" sciences, theoretical generalization is difficult from findings based on any social science research design, but in principle it is no more difficult from a case study than from large-sample research, and it is possible in both. The idea of physical causality is a critical element in reaching this conclusion.

The configuration of this book's topics follows straightforwardly from the goals and premises set out at the beginning of the introduction. Chapters 1 and 2 take up the question of causation, critiquing the common existing views and developing the dual definition—physical and factual causality—to take their place. The original counterfactual definition is given special attention because it has been the most explicitly and recently defended interpretation of causation for the social sciences. Given the usual requirements for a valid definition, the counterfactual view fails because of four serious problems, yet in spirit it does capture a salient meaning of causation. "Factual causality" modifies the traditional counterfactual view so that it retains its basic meaning but is no longer vulnerable to any of the four criticisms. The modification succeeds, however, only on the basis of a rigorous defense of the notion of physical causality. To support the validity of physical causation, in turn, it is necessary to show that Hume's rejection of the idea too hastily passed over an important possibility—an epistemological foundation in the sense of touch rather than that of vision.

Chapter 3 concerns itself primarily with the affect-object paradigm—a view of the physiological mechanism that generates intentional behavior. Armed with the findings from the first two chapters, I give special attention to the possible causal role of thoughts, reasons, and affect, with the conclusions that are sketched briefly in the questions and answers above.

The balance of the book—chapters 4 through 6—treats the implications of the findings on causation and the causal mechanism that generates behavior for a number of salient issues in modern social science research methods. These include (*a*) the kinds of causal reasoning that must be built into social science research designs, (*b*) the relative power of large-sample designs, small-sample designs, and the case study, (*c*) the contrasting possibilities for causal explanation and lawlike explanation in social science, (*d*) the form that theoretical generalization must take, and (*e*) the implications of many of these issues for two current theoretical approaches that are meant to be all-encompassing— namely, the rational choice approach and the accepted approach to the explanation of behavior in evolutionary biology.

Chapter 1

Factual Cause

My overall objective is to arrive at several new positions in the methodology of social science, primarily through an examination of the concept of causation and the mechanism that generates intentional human behavior. We begin with issues of causation.

We will see in the ensuing discussion that there is no definition of causality in the current literature—either of social science or philosophy—that is able to avoid serious conceptual problems. I judge that the dominant definition in philosophy at present is still the Humean definition, in spite of considerable discussion of interesting alternatives (see Beauchamp 1974; Sosa 1975). I will examine that definition in detail below as it concerns social science. Suffice it to say here, however, that under the Humean view, primarily because of its reliance on universal laws as the basis of causal knowledge, the very relevance of causation to social science is problematic. It is possible that the term in this view is simply illegitimate. If this is true, what would it mean? It would mean, for example, that a claim such as "Hamilton's ideas had a strong effect on the Constitution" would be dubious in principle because "to have an effect" is just one of the many ways of saying "to cause," and it is extremely doubtful whether the relation between Hamilton's ideas and the Constitution can be subsumed under a general law—particularly of the observable sort that Hume had in mind. If such sentences were illegitimate, the problem would be a serious one, for if Hamilton's ideas (or Madison's or Franklin's) were not a cause of the behavior that determined the content of the Constitution, it must be that his ideas and the Constitution were similar by pure coincidence. I claim that there is no other way than coincidence by which they could possibly be related once the causation of behavior is removed from the picture.

Such a state of affairs would not be tolerable. We appear to use the term *cause* meaningfully in ordinary conversation about human behavior. Why not legitimately in social research as well? One reason for this

13

unsatisfactory situation, perhaps, is that much of the philosophical discussion of causation has been rooted in the needs and characteristics of physics. The concept has an uncomfortable existence even there, but those problems aside, social science needs a conceptualization of its own—one that fits the needs of the study of human behavior. It is the aim of this chapter and the next to develop such a conceptualization.

The Counterfactual Definition

A definition that apparently fits our needs much better than the Humean view is the necessary condition or counterfactual definition (I will use the two labels interchangeably). It is not common for methodological essays in social science to set out explicitly the conceptualization of causation on which their treatment and perspectives are based, but at least one recent and careful book, by King et al. (1994), cites the elaboration of the counterfactual definition by Holland (1986) and uses it as the foundation for its treatment of important methodological issues. Philosophers have also elaborated and defended the counterfactual definition (see Mackie 1980; Lewis 1973).

This definition states that X was a cause of Y if and only if X was a necessary condition; if not X, then not Y. To say, for example, that "the desperate need for increased productivity was a cause of their adoption of the new robotics" means: if there had been no desperate need, there would have been no adoption of the innovation. Let us appraise this definition carefully since it is apparently critical for the possibility of causal explanation in social science. To carry out the appraisal, we need standards for definitions. The terminology just used—*if and only if X was a necessary condition*—states and applies the usual criteria for the validity of a conceptual definition or, as those in philosophy would put it, an "analysis." This definition would fail on the "if" criterion, in other words, if there were cases in which X was indeed a necessary condition but we are nevertheless unwilling to consider it a cause, and it would fail on the "only if" criterion if there were cases in which we agree that X was a cause but can see that it was not a necessary condition. In addition to the if-and-only-if criterion, any definition must fail if it is circular. This is an important standard in the present instance, for we will see that allowing the concept itself to slip into definitions of the concept plagues the study of causation.

On these standard criteria, the counterfactual definition is seriously flawed. The general idea makes a good deal of sense, but the definition needs to be modified in a fundamental way in order to be workable. Thus modified, I claim that it is indeed workable but only as part of a joint or dual definition of causation. The dual definition, I propose, stands as a valid analysis of the concept of causation, weathering all criticisms of which I am aware, and helping as well to clarify some critical factors pertinent to explanation, laws, theory, design, and method in the social sciences. Let me present what I consider to be the best elaboration of the standard counterfactual definition from the standpoint of utility in social science, largely based on Mackie (1980), and proceed to point out its deficiencies.

First, we presume that X and Y both occurred, that is, there was a desperate need for increased productivity, and there was likewise the adoption of the robotics innovation. Next, in saying that X was a cause of Y we are saying that X was a necessary condition: if X had not occurred, then neither would Y. We also stipulate that X and Y must be distinct existences; that is, we rule out such claims as "The acorn (X) caused the tree (Y)" and "Landing on heads (X) caused the coin not to land on tails (Y)" even though, in both cases, X was necessary for Y. But further, we specify that X must have been necessary *in the circumstances*. By this critical stipulation we mean the following: consider everything in the world to have been exactly as it actually was, so that all of the conditions for bringing about Y or not bringing it about were in place. These are the "circumstances." Now imagine that, given those very circumstances, X had not occurred. If and only if in that case Y would not have occurred, then X was a cause of Y. One might have suggested, for example, that the desperate need was not necessary and therefore was not a cause—that the innovation would have been adopted anyway even if there had been no desperate need—because the new plant manager was infatuated with gadgetry, because the organization wanted by this means to increase its prestige in the industry, or because serious personnel difficulties could only be remedied by the radical reassignment occasioned by such a change. Many such considerations might presumably motivate an organization to adopt a technological innovation. The fact of the matter is, however, whether or not we have any way of knowing it, that such things either were true of the organization in question or they were not. To say that X was a cause, that X was necessary in the circumstances, means that these other considerations were not in place and about to cause the adoption of this innovation at this time. In our circumstances, let us say, the world was such that this organization did not even have a new plant manager, felt no pressure to increase its already towering prestige, and had no unusual personnel difficulties to speak of. In fact, let us also say that if the world had run on normally in the wake of the precise preexisting circumstances but without the desperate need for increased productivity, then the organization would not have adopted the new robotics. In that case, and only in that case, was the desperate need a cause.

I will note four technical problems, each of which incapacitates the counterfactual definition as it now stands for use as the designated definition of causality in social science. Moreover, and I wish to emphasize this point, in each case we will see that there is apparently an underlying or "naive" view of causation that we all tend to use and against which we test the results of applying the counterfactual definition. I think it is plain that this naive view is a view of "physical" causation, and I will in any case claim that such a view is both fundamental and defensible.

By physical causation I mean the intuitive notion of mechanical connection. Cause for most of us, at least much of the time, is readily understood as a pushing or pulling or lifting or smashing and so on. The definition would seem to be a simple one. It is not an accepted one, however, because in the 1730s Hume disabused us of the notion that we ever could define causality in this mechanical sense, and his penetrating critique of the idea remains highly influential to the present day. Hume's point (1955) was that a power or necessity connecting one object with another, the cause with the effect, could never be observed per se. All that we can see is that one event follows another. After all, what substance, mechanism, or power can we see in common to label "cause" when (*a*) a magnet attracts a nail toward itself and (*b*) a hammer drives a nail into a board? Hume challenged his contemporaries to answer such questions by documenting and explaining their observations of the objects, and his challenge has never been met. Nevertheless, I have found in my own extensive discussions (and so did Hume, as we will see) a general readiness to accept this notion of cause as valid whether it is philosophically tenable or not. In this chapter, I will treat the intuitive view of physical causation as though it were conceptually sound and defensible. In the following chapter, I will elaborate the concept more rigorously and defend it against the Humean and other critiques.

Four Technical Problems

The counterfactual definition is severely challenged by the problems of redundancy, collateral effects, the distinction between "make-happen" and "let-happen" causes, and circularity. We first review the issue of *redundancy*, a problem that is illustrated by many intriguing and colorful examples of overdetermination, preemption, and other variants in the pertinent literature (e.g., Mackie 1965, 1980: 44–48; Loeb 1974; Katz 1987: 210–51). We will consider three kinds of cases in connection with this first general problem, each in some depth. Note that most of the examples used for illustration in this section are simple and might seem on the surface to have little to do with social science. The counterfactual definition, however, is a definition of causation in the single instance. It does not depend on generalizations of any sort (in spite of the fact, as we will see here and in chapter 4, that it is the foundation of experimental and similar research designs as well as of any statistical approach to causation). To test the definition, therefore, it is well to test it primarily on its basic home ground, the singular causal statement.

In the first example of redundancy, we start the machine by pushing the "on" button with two thumbs simultaneously, yours and mine, whereas one alone would easily have done the job. Neither thumb was necessary in the circumstances, so that, by the counterfactual definition, neither was a cause of the machine's beginning to operate. This is an uncomfortable conclusion because our intuitive notions of physical causation and the ways of machinery tell us with certainty that something caused the machine to start and that both of these thumbs were somehow implicated. Thus, the necessary condition definition of causation has itself failed to be necessary—that is, it has failed on the "only if" criterion for valid definitions (here, only if the thumb were necessary was it a cause)—in that we have here a factor (pressure from the thumb) that was not necessary in the circumstances but was nevertheless a cause. The same is true of all of the varieties of redundancy to follow. It is also true, and noteworthy, that our naive view from the perspective of physical causation (pressure by the thumb was a cause) seems to emerge as more trustworthy in this instance than the counterfactual definition. Partisans of that definition should begin here to face this fact and act accordingly by relaxing a total reliance on the counter-factual definition and seeking instead for ways to salvage the utility that it obviously has.

Let us bring the same problem closer to home with a social science example (suggested by an example in King, et al. 1994). In a survey of women in the work force, respondents were found to fall into three categories: (*a*) the respondent went to college but her parents did not; (*b*) the respondent did not go to college but her parents did; and (*c*) both the respondent and her parents went to college. For the group of respondents in each of these three categories, the mean and variance of income turned out to be the same. We introduce here a notion that we will return to later on, namely, that in quantitative approaches, certain categories of observed subjects function as the basis for estimating the outcome for other observed subjects under the counterfactual. Here, for example, "if not X," where X is the parents' college, is represented or estimated by the category in which the parents did not go to college—group (a). Let us focus now on group (c), in which both respondent and parents went to college, and ask whether either factor was a cause of the resulting income levels in that group. Given the estimates of the counterfactuals that we have from groups (a) and (b), we see that neither the respondents' going to college nor their parents' doing so was necessary to produce the levels of income recorded when they did go to college, so that neither was a cause by the counterfactual definition. Correspondingly, regression analysis would yield zero coefficients. Yet intuitively we would insist that both may indeed have been causes. If they happened not to be, it was for reasons other than those indicated by the zero coefficients or, equivalently, for reasons having nothing to do with the demonstration that these factors were not necessary in the circumstances.

If we had data on people who did not go to college and whose parents also did not, we would observe nonzero regression coefficients, but those individuals would answer a different question. They would not supply evidence for the counterfactual pertinent to the particular individuals in group (c) under the criterion we have called "in the circumstances." The relevant circumstances for those in group (c) who went to college, for example, include the fact that their parents also went to college. Under those circumstances, our best estimate is that their income would have been the same had they themselves not attended, so that their attending was not necessary and was not a cause, and the same is symmetrically true for parents' attending. The problem is one of overkill or redundancy, just as in the case of the two thumbs.

As a second example of the problem of redundancy, consider a kind of case that has been important for jurisprudence (Mackie 1980: 44; Katz 1987: 210–51): Alphonse puts poison in Henri's canteen but, unaware of this, Gaston sneaks in later and makes a very small hole in it. The (poisoned) water leaks out and the evidently unpopular Henri dies of thirst while crossing the desert. Alphonse did not cause Henri's death because the poison was never drunk, but we must say that neither did Gaston because the puncture was not necessary in the circumstances. The poison was set to do the job if the puncture had not. Whether Gaston should be punished for this death, and if so how severely, is perhaps a complicated matter, but he does appear to have been some sort of cause; the physical connection between the puncture and the death is evident and is how we establish the causal relation. We do so, however, in spite of the clear conclusion derived from the counterfactual definition that Gaston's puncture was not necessary.

As a final type of redundancy, consider what has been called "preemption" (Lewis 1973): Annie is about to stumble on a rock but fortunately Manny and Fanny both yell "Look out!" at the same time. Fanny has such a soft voice that Annie hears only Manny. However, if Manny had said nothing, thereby not drowning Fanny out, then Annie would have heard Fanny and so would have jumped precisely as she did do to keep herself from falling down. Surely, Fanny is not the cause of Annie's jumping, but neither must Manny's role be considered causal since it was not necessary in the circumstances. Physically, we would say without hesitation that "Annie heard Manny," and it is by this means that we know that the counterfactual definition, which assigns the causal role to no one at all in this case, has failed.

The following is a similar case, and I will lean more heavily on it as we continue the critique because it is more closely related to topics in social science research. The physical aspects, by the way, will not presently be so clear in this case because the example deals with somewhat more complicated kinds of human behavior, but it is a major aim of the present volume to clarify the physical causal aspects of human behavior, thus permitting it to be comprehended completely by the general doctrine of causation. We will return to that task in subsequent chapters. The case: Both the secretary of state and the national security advisor write a memorandum to the president containing an idea for taking advantage of a fast-breaking crisis in a South American country. In the spirit of rules of thumb worked out in the administration, the White House chief of staff forwards the secretary of state's memorandum to the president but suppresses the one from the national security advisor. In such matters, *if* State displays an active concern, the National Security Council is to remain in the wings until its advice is sought. The president reads the memo from State and takes steps to implement the policy idea. The cause of his taking these steps is surely not the memorandum from the national security advisor, but neither must the memorandum from the secretary of state be considered causal since it was not necessary in the circumstances. The counterfactual definition has failed because of the preemptive form of redundancy. Physically, we detect the failure because it is overwhelmingly evident that the president read the memo from State, just as Annie clearly heard Manny. What is left for later discussion is the less obvious causal connection between the president's reading the memo and taking the subsequent action.

It is perhaps possible to rescue the counterfactual definition from the challenge of the second case by insisting that it was Gaston's puncture that caused the particular kind of death that occurred: whereas Henri would have died anyway, the death that was actually caused was death by thirst, for which the puncture actually was necessary. Even if this escape were to be accepted, however, and I will claim that it should not be, the first and third cases are fatal (the solution offered by Lewis [1973] for the case of preemption—which I find problematic—will be reviewed below). In both, the counterfactual definition leaves us with the highly unsatisfactory conclusion that certain factors were not causes, contrary to our best considered judgment.

Next, we note the second technical problem, that of *collateral effects*. In the abstract, consider whether X is the cause of Y if there is a third factor, W, that is necessary and sufficient in the circumstances both for X and Y. To use an example from Mackie (1980: 33), the Tories win (W), which pleases James (X) and saddens John (Y). The two men do not know each other and have no contact, and let us also stipulate for the sake of purity that James received the news first. Did James's being pleased cause John to be sad? Using the counterfactual definition, one is required to say yes.

Before elaborating, we need to understand the stipulation "sufficient for" as I have used it here. I mean "sufficient in the strong sense" (Mackie 1980: 39–44). If we refer to a law or regularity when we say that W is sufficient for Y, we mean that every time W occurs, so does Y. But if we refer only to a single instance, as here, what can "sufficient" mean except that W occurred and Y occurred (which we already know from an element of the counterfactual definition)? This sense of "sufficient" is too weak. Instead, we give it the strong sense: *If not Y, then not W.* For example, to say that flipping the switch in these circumstances was sufficient in the strong sense for the light's going on, we mean that if the light had not gone on then the switch simply was not flipped. (One might think of it in this way: as long as the light has not gone on, one knows for sure that the switch has not been flipped.) Thus, we are supposing in assuming that W was sufficient for X and Y that if John had not been sad, or by the same token if James had not been pleased, then the Tories could not have won the election—for if the Tories had, then James and John surely would have been pleased and sad, respectively. The Tories' victory was sufficient in the strong sense.

We must, then, say that James's being pleased was necessary for John's being sad, satisfying the counterfactual definition of causation, because if James had not been pleased, then the Tories could not have won, and if they had not, then John would not be sad, so that if not X then not Y. James must therefore be considered a cause in this view, and the counterfactual definition therefore fails on the "if" or sufficiency criterion: X was necessary; nevertheless, it was not a cause. (Possible solutions offered by Mackie [1980] and Lewis [1973] will be reviewed below. However, they do not appear to me to mend the flaw.)

This is not a minor or picky problem. Survey researchers recognize it immediately as the counterpart in the single instance to the problem of "spurious causation." If the variables X and Y are related in survey research, as for example attending college and turning out to vote, then it is possible that a third factor—socioeconomic status, perhaps—was responsible for the relationship by causing both. Not only does the *threat* of spuriousness always hang over relationships in survey research, it is well known to be actualized much of the time, so that the investigator tries to measure and control statistically for all potential sources of spuriousness that can be foreseen (leaving always, unfortunately, the threat of those not imagined). Clearly, we do not want to label the attending college variable as causal when in fact it was not. That is why the labels "spurious" and "partly spurious" are used instead. But under the counterfactual definition, *we must* label it as causal, and that need becomes a crushing incapacity for the definition.

Note once more that you and I are wiser than the definition. That is, we know that James did *not* cause John to be sad, even though it is true that if James had not been pleased, John would not have been sad. To know this, we must have a sense of the meaning of causation to begin with, one that, we now recognize, the counterfactual definition does not completely capture. What we should do perhaps is to try to bring into the open the definition that we really use and see whether that holds consistently. I suggest again that we know James was not the cause, and have little if any doubt about this, because we believe that there was no physical linkage of any conceivable sort—touching, hearing, or hearing about; direct or indirect; forcing, enabling, or facilitating—between James's being pleased and John's being sad.

After the various forms of redundancy and collateral effects, the third technical problem is the failure of the counterfactual definition to *distinguish the "make-happen" from the "let-happen" sense of causality*—like collateral effects, a failure on the "if" or sufficiency criterion for a definition. Consider that someone opened the shutter irresponsibly, and a ball broke the window. Both of these factors were causes but in different senses. Intuitively, we know the difference. The ball was a cause in a direct, physical, mechanical sense as well as being a necessary condition, whereas opening the shutter was a cause *only* in the necessary condition sense, but not more. We recognize the difference in ordinary language in that we would (and did) say that the ball "broke" the window but would not say that opening the shutter broke the window. In fact, if we were to say that someone broke the window by opening the shutter we would mean something quite different from what happened in this case. The distinction stands out vividly when we think of make-happen and let-happen causes in the perspective of causal laws. Such laws have to do with the physical universe, so that only make-happen causes are subsumed under them. If we say that if he had not touched the high voltage line he would not have been electrocuted, we know that the central event is subsumable under a causal law, but if we say that if he had not walked home by that route he would not have been electrocuted, no causal law subsumes the relation; and the same difference holds between the ball and the shutter. If we recognize the distinction, we must have a further or compound definition to comprehend the more specialized category, narrowed to feature make-happen causes, or else we have nothing at all to conceptualize a nuance of causation that we freely invoke. Thus, the counterfactual definition is not sufficient to cover make-happen or physical causality, just as the legal definition of "assault" is not sufficient to cover "aggravated assault" or "felonious assault." If we insist on exclusive reliance on the counterfactual definition, we merely sweep this interesting distinction among causes under the rug.

Last, for the fourth technical problem, the counterfactual definition fails on the *circularity criterion;* it begs the question. Assume for stark simplicity that there are only two possible causes of some effect, as, for example, the secretary of state's memorandum and the national security advisor's. We might suppose that we can conclude that the secretary of state's memorandum was causal because we know that if it had not occurred, then neither would Y. But what enables us to say that Y would not? The answer always is our view that in the circumstances, nothing *else* was set to cause Y. Note, however, the circular and therefore illicit mention of "cause" here. In a deterministic universe, to say that Y would not occur is to say precisely that nothing would cause Y, so that the counterfactual definition is now seen to be the circular statement: X caused Y if and only if X and Y both occurred and, if X had not occurred, then nothing would have caused Y.

Such, then, are the shortcomings of causes as necessary conditions. It is desirable and indeed possible to modify the definition to overcome all of these challenges, but the modification, though simple in appearance, involves a fundamental change in the formal conceptualization of causation.

Moving to Factual Causation

I have suggested that a notion of physical causation is prior to and underlies our sense of causation as rendered by the counterfactual definition. We use it to test whether that definition truly is necessary and sufficient for our sense of causality, and we also find it popping up as a background sense of causality when the definition turns out to be circular. One might therefore suppose that a switch from the counterfactual definition to pure physical causation itself would be in order. That will not do for social science, however, because a physical or make-happen definition would leave out too much of importance that is commonly referred to as "cause" in research—as well as in common usage.

Completely omitted, for example, would be all let-happen causes, such as opening the shutter or, let us say, raising the speed limit to 70 miles per hour, which might well be seen as a cause—but not a physical cause—of a rise in highway fatalities. Completely excluded as well would be the causation of things that did not happen, as, for example, "The president was not assassinated only because the route of the motorcade was changed." A third kind of omission would be the widely prevalent and conceptually crucial category of probabilistic encounters, on which, I will show, all intentional behavior depends but which cannot be physically caused. Last, there is a wide array of concepts and relations that could indeed be reduced to physical cause and effect but are not thought of or written about in that form. Suppose one asked, for example, "What caused Yellowstone to become one of our most popular national parks?" This "becoming popular" is not, as it stands, the kind of effect that takes a physical cause, but we might want to explain it causally even so and without reducing it to elements of individual behaviors in the mass public. In the same way, to say that careful planning by the chair caused the meeting to "run smoothly," that democratic supervision was responsible for "high morale," or that the approach of Christmas caused "heavy traffic"—is to refer to effects that are not, as they stand, ordinary physical effects. These statements of relationship that are empirical but are not instances of physical causality are "factual" in their essence in that they deal, as Strawson points out (1985: 115), with statements, facts, and truths rather than with two entities that existed in nature and the natural relation between them. We basically must say that the *fact* that the chair of the committee planned so well caused the *fact* that the meeting ran smoothly, and so on.

Thus, I suggest that "cause" is regularly meant in two senses—the concept is implemented in two ways. We have, first, physical cause and, second, factual cause. It is critical in maintaining clarity and avoiding confusion that these two senses of causality be kept distinct, but we cannot dispense with either one. We have these two senses, I further suggest, because the idea is used for two purposes. Factual cause is used primarily to assign responsibility, as in simple explanation, or in explanation with a moral cast—blame, praise, credit, fault, guilt, and so forth. The purpose of physical cause, on the other hand, is simply to describe the physical workings of the world, as in science, medicine, cause-of-death coding, engineering, and storytelling. Physical and factual causation are thus fundamentally different from one another in concept and have distinct uses. Nonetheless, we will see that they are intimately related.

When we seek clarification either of how we know causation when it happens or of what people mean by the term when they use it, then the definition is disjunctive (either/or); that is, we *know* causation when it occurs (the epistemic function of the definition) by virtue of applying either the physical or the factual analysis, or both. And what we *mean* by cause (the conceptual function) is cause either in the physical sense or the factual sense or both. To the extent that a definition tries to get at the nature of the phenomenon as it exists in the world (the ontological function), only physical cause is pertinent—factual cause being a relation between statements rather than natural events—and pending some long-awaited and probably far-off discoveries in physics, even the physical definition can at this point be only indicative and not precisely descriptive.

Encounters

I noted in an earlier book that a good deal of prominent scientific work, including both Mendelian and Darwinian theory, is pointed toward the theoretical explanation of *encounters* rather than of simpler events (see "process theory" in Mohr 1982: 44–70). It is now clear that the difference between this type of theory and the type that is featured in Newtonian physics is linked significantly to the two conceptions of causality in common use: certain natural events are physically caused; encounters, however, can only be factually caused. With this distinction we will also be able to see why there can be no universal laws of human behavior and why human science must differ in that regard from physical science.

A probabilistic encounter is a compound event conceptualized as the status relative to each other of two or more free, component objects or events. By "free" I mean the opposite of a given or of a fixed frame of reference. For example, when we speak of a motion upward or downward, we mean relative to the earth, but the earth is taken as a fixed frame of reference, so that this motion is simply the motion of an object and not an encounter. Similarly, the collision of two billiard balls on a table is an encounter, but the motion of one of them afterward is simply the motion of an object. It is not an encounter involving the ball and the table because the table is taken as a fixed frame of reference.

An automobile accident—a collision between two cars—is an example of a probabilistic encounter. If we conceptualized an event as two ships passing in the night, that would be an encounter in just the same way. We will see that physical causation has to do fundamentally with the motion of single objects as effects. The accident and the passing as such, however, are not motions of one or more objects but rather a juxtaposition of things—a status of things relative to one another. The specific forces involved impinged physically on *each* of the cars or ships, but none of these forces produced the accident or passing per se.

On the other hand, encounters do have factual causes, and when we talk about the causes of encounters, which we very frequently do, this is what we have in mind. In the circumstances, the first driver's sneezing was a cause of the accident in the counterfactual sense as was the second driver's going through a red light, because, we may suppose, without each of these the accident would never have occurred.

The reader will be aware in the discussion that follows that encounters may often be physically *explained*, at least in part, even if technically they are not physically caused. For example, the arrival of *each* car at the exact location of the accident at a particular time is an event with a full background of physical causation, and the accident may then be explained by invoking the pair of separate but constituent causal streams, that is, by deciding to take both of them into account simultaneously. Granting this—and in fact I will emphasize the point—it is still of critical importance that encounters per se are not physically caused. Unless we see encounters as a special category, particularly in this regard, I believe we will lose ready access to important insights in social science. Encounters are an important enough category to warrant their being viewed in several perspectives and especially as the targets of explanation by factual causality.

Winning at roulette is an encounter between a certain bet and the stopping place of a little ball. Because it is not something that receives a force and that moves, the "winning" has no physical cause. It is very common for events to be conceptualized as encounters. Thus, encounters represent a huge category of events in the world that may be targets of explanation in social science but that are not physically caused. The following are some additional examples: a tie for first place, solo possession of first place, bumping into an old friend, stumbling over a root, getting caught in the rain, agreement, job satisfaction, and so forth.

One important function of encounters is to serve as a link connecting two or more causal instances, so that series linked in this fashion are therefore factual causal chains. Suppose that I leave poisoned meat and a coyote comes upon it, eats it, and dies. We would often say that my behavior was the cause of the coyote's death, but it is surely not so by virtue of a continuous chain of physical causality. The series under consideration here is bridged by a number of encounters, one of the primary ones being the encounter of the coyote with the meat. The series that focuses on the process of one of the car's getting into the accident is similarly punctuated by encounters all along the line and is significantly affected as well by encounters that are conceptualized as nonoccurrences. For example, the encounter of the car with a smooth road all the way is most importantly a nonoccurrence, that is, it is an encounter of the car with *the alternative to* a large pothole or the jagged shard of a broken bottle. Finally, note that a general function of encounters in a causal chain is to transfer the flow of causation from one element of the encounter to another, so that the chain does not simply die out. The poison lies in my hand until it encounters the meat, then in the meat until the encounter with the coyote, then in certain parts of the coyote until the digestive system puts it in contact with other parts, and so forth.

The Definition

The following, then, is the proposed definition: X was the factual cause of Y if and only if X and Y both occurred and X occupied a necessary slot in the physical causal scenario pertinent to Y. For the most part, the standard counterfactual definition captures the spirit of factual causation well. The shift from a necessary *event*, such as X, to a necessary *slot*, or function, is in most instances a minor one. The basis of the claim that something is necessary, however, and the basis of the recognition that it is indeed X that fills a certain slot are inaccessible to the standard counterfactual definition. The modified version, on the other hand, has ready, valid access to these claims and thereby is able to manage well the four technical challenges on which the standard definition was seen to founder.

Finally, the language of the definition as just given is informal for convenience but may be elaborated more rigorously as follows: From our knowledge of physical causation, chains of causation, and the physical configuration of the world at the time of X, we know that at least k instances of physical causation resulting in various outcomes Y_i, $i = 1, \ldots, k$, had to occur just as they did in order for Y to occur just as it did. Either X was the physical cause of one of the Y_i or the implied alternative to X, call it "not X," would have been the physical cause of not Y_i. (To clarify the latter, if X is opening the shutter, for example, and Y_i is entering the air space between the shutter and the window, then opening the shutter [X] was not literally the physical cause of the ball's entering the air space [Y_i], but the closed shutter ["not X"] would have been the physical cause of the ball's being diverted from that air space [not Y_i].)

In the balance of this section, I will present several examples to clarify the application of the modified definition, taking some general cases first and then proceeding to the particular kinds of cases that have traditionally made life difficult for the counterfactual analysis of causality.

Hamilton and the Constitution. To put the causal claim in language that makes it clear that it is factual causation we are talking about and not physical, we would say, "The fact that Hamilton articulated certain ideas (X) caused the fact that the Constitution had certain content (Y). The physical causal scenario pertinent to Y is the collection of natural events leading up to and including the taking of certain behaviors by the framers of the Constitution, behaviors that amounted to giving the Constitution certain parts of its content. What caused the framers to take these behaviors? There is a physical, behavior-generating mechanism in the body, one whose nature is important for the argument being developed here. We will consider it explicitly in chapter 3, but nothing is lost in the present context by assuming any particular form, so let us suppose that the mechanism may be summed up by the causal use of such terms as reasons or decisions. Reasons or decisions, then, caused the framers' behavior, but in order for them to have had the reasons or have come to the decisions they did, the neuronal processing of certain information, experiences, ideas, and so forth was physically necessary. The original causal claim is true, then, if ideas emanating from Hamilton were among these and false if they were not. It is important to note in this first example that *we need not show Hamilton's ideas to have been necessary in the sense of the counterfactual definition*. The factual causal claim is still true even if, in the actual circumstances, ideas serving precisely the same purpose would have gotten into the framers' heads anyway in the event that Hamilton's had not. What is determinative is that *some* information had to play this role (a "necessary slot"), and Hamilton's ideas either were or were not the ones that actually, physically did. If they were, then we are able to say in the factual causal sense that Hamilton's ideas had an effect on the Constitution. Thus, the traditional counterfactual definition might fail, but the modified one would not. Moreover, the latter's success depends on the prior acceptance of physical causation, or else we would have no way of saying that "Hamilton's ideas . . . were . . . the ones that actually, physically did" cause certain neurons to fire, let us say. Instead, we would always have had recourse only to the counterfactual "If Hamilton's had not . . . ," which is ineffectual in this case.

The 70-mph Speed Limit. I use this example to explicate let-happen causation. There is no technical improvement here over the counterfactual definition, but I hope to give some concreteness to the reasons why a counterfactual approach does work in the case of let-happen causes. The factual causal claim here is to the effect that "The fact that the speed limit was raised to 70 miles per hour (X) caused the fact that the highway fatality rate increased (Y)." What we have in the physical causal scenario is a lot of people dying, presumably because they or others were driving at high speeds in response to certain motives. Thus, the new speed limit did not *make* people drive fast. If it is nevertheless involved, it is involved as a let-happen cause. Let-happen causes appear in the scenario as what we have referred to as "the circumstances." Such a circumstance is causal if, had it been otherwise—had it been the particular not X that it would otherwise have been—the causal chain would have been interrupted or diverted and Y would not have eventuated, just as in the case of the closed shutter. Here, if the speed law had been 55 miles per hour as it used to be, a concern about moral uprightness or getting caught would have overpowered the motives behind driving fast in many cases and certain deaths would not have occurred. The 70-mph speed limit occupied a necessary slot because the speeding regulation in effect at the time had to be something other than a 55-mph limit in order for the additional deaths to occur, and a 70-mph limit is the content that the regulation actually had.

The following is a related example in which X was something that did *not* occur (whereas the 70-mph speed limit did): "If Kerensky had thrown Lenin into jail, the Bolshevik revolution would not have occurred," that is, not throwing Lenin into jail was a let-happen cause of the revolution's taking place. The analysis follows the same line as the previous example and is even more transparent.

Nonoccurrence. The nonoccurrence of Y is somewhat more troublesome than the nonoccurrence of X. "The fact that the route of the motorcade was changed (X) caused the fact that the president was not assassinated (Y)." In the physical causal scenario as it actually played itself out, the president did *other* things at the time of Y rather than encounter a bullet on the original route—in particular, he rode down Mulberry Avenue. This is the scenario pertinent to Y because it contains the things the president actually did at the time of Y that made it physically impossible that he did Y. We look, in the explanation of nonoccurrences, for let-happen causes that act as switches or gates mediating between the actual scenario (Mulberry Avenue) and the nonoccurrence that concerns us (being assassinated). The changing of the route was such a let-happen cause in that, had the route not been changed, this would have switched the causal flow away from Mulberry Avenue and, in the circumstances, toward the encounter with the bullet instead.

The President and the Secretary of State. The troublesome case of redundancy of this sort has already been settled in the example of Hamilton and the Constitution. For example, something had to alert Annie in order for the physical causal scenario to play itself out, and Manny happened to be it. Similarly, something had to give the president the idea, and the secretary of state's memorandum happened to be it. Thus, in spite of the fact that the secretary of state's memorandum was not necessary, it did in fact physically occupy a slot that was necessary and therefore was a cause. The example once more emphasizes the importance of physical causation in the concept of factual cause. The term *occupy* in the definition is seen to be equally as important as the term *necessary*. With the ordinary counterfactual definition, there is no way to allow oneself to focus on reality. We might say that *someone* had to write a memorandum in order for the president to read the idea, and the secretary of state did so, but remember that the national security advisor did so as well. We are frustrated in not being able to use the information we clearly have that it was the secretary of state's memorandum that actually played the critical role, *even though it was not necessary.* In pinning the definition to the occupation of a slot in a physical scenario, we invoke the actual instances of physical causation that occurred in the chain between someone's writing a memorandum and the president's taking steps to implement the policy. It is this that enables us to select the secretary of state, and this is not available in the standard, counterfactual perspective.

Lewis (1973) offers a solution within the counterfactual tradition that also invokes a causal chain, but by his counterfactual-based definition of causation it must be a chain of counterfactuals rather than one that focuses on physical causation, as here (see Loeb 1974). That is, X was a cause of Y if and only if there was an unbroken chain of two or more counterfactuals leading from X to Y. Lewis's claim would be that whereas there was no chain of counterfactuals leading from the national security advisor to the ultimate outcome, there was such a chain leading from the secretary of state. I believe, however, that the claim is problematic. A complete rendering of the sort of chain Lewis has in mind is the following: If the secretary of state had not written, then the president would not have read his memorandum, and if he had not read it, then he would not have taken steps to implement it. By this chain of counterfactuals—if not X then not Z, and if not Z then not Y—the secretary of state's memorandum emerges as a true cause. The obvious objection is that, at the second stage, if the president did not read the secretary of state's memorandum (not Z), then going backward, the latter must not have written it (not X), in which case the chief of staff would have forwarded the national security advisor's memorandum, and the president would have taken steps to implement the policy anyway. In this light (because we cannot say that if the president had not read the memorandum from state he would not have acted), as in the original statement of the problem, counterfactual reasoning fails to make the secretary of state a cause. To this objection Lewis replies that there is no need to go all the way back to the secretary of state's writing the memorandum (X) and eliminate that in order to account for the president's not having read it (not Z). It is less of a violation of physical laws and the stipulation of circumstances in the case to change something closer to the time of reading. For example, we might suppose at the second stage that if the president had not read the memo from state it was because the chief of staff, not liking the idea himself, suppressed both of the memos.

Here, however, we have been asked to take one step too far into the realm of the hypothetical. If we suppose for the sake of the chain of counterfactuals that the president did not read the secretary of state's memorandum, Lewis's account forces us also to *suppose* some additional violation of the original circumstances to account for it. That necessity is fatal because it avows our *uncertainty* about what would happen to the outcome in case the counterfactual (not Z) were true. We can make up anything. One possibility to account for the president's not reading the memo from State is to suppose that the secretary of state did not write a memorandum at all. As just reviewed, that leads us to eliminate the secretary of state as a cause (since the president would have read about the idea anyway). Another, and the sort of alternative that Lewis favors, is to suppose that the chief of staff suppressed both memos because he himself did not like the idea. That is, the secretary of state wrote and the president read his memorandum, and if he had not read the secretary of state's memorandum (because the chief of staff suppressed both of them), he would not have taken steps to implement the policy (noting that he also would not have heard from the national security advisor). This alternative *does* make the secretary of state a cause. A third possibility, however (and one that is even closer to the time of reading), is to suppose that the president was listening to a newscast when the memorandum from State was placed before him and heard the very same idea from the commentator, which totally distracted him from further reading. That is, the secretary of state wrote and the president read his memo, and if he had not read that memo (because of the distraction of the newscast), he would have taken steps to implement the policy anyway. This leads us once more to eliminate the secretary of state as a cause. Which of these three alternative violations of the circumstances, or any of a hundred others, shall we select to represent the case? The correct answer, I submit, is that we have no right to select any of them.

The fact is that the consequence (in terms of Y—taking steps to implement the policy) of the president's counterfactual failure to read the secretary of state's memorandum is *uncertain* given the original realities of the case. To use an ordinary counterfactual argument, one varies the potential cause (if X had not occurred, . . .) and jumps to a conclusion with certainty about the potential effect (. . . neither would Y). (Where this certainty could possibly come from suggests the fourth of the previously noted technical flaws in the counterfactual definition of causality. Let us permit ourselves, however, to leave aside this other flaw while we discuss redundancy and allow in this context the certainty about Y that is generally assumed.) In Lewis's attempt to save the counterfactual definition, however, uncertainty about Y is explicitly introduced. In that case, the argument about what *would* have happened simply fails. We are not able to say that if the middle link had not occurred (i.e., if the president had not read the memo from State), then Y *would* not have occurred. We can say only that it *might* not have, depending on what factor we select to *account* for the counterfactual on the middle link. And to say that Y might not have occurred cannot be enough to make X a cause.

Two Thumbs; College and Income. "The fact that my thumb pushed on the button (X) caused the fact that the machine started (Y)." The problem is that you were pushing at the same time. Physically, when you did so, the two forces commingled in the rigid button, so as to become unidentifiable components of one force. Therefore, neither you nor I was the physical cause, but each of us was part of a total physical cause. Was my part necessary? In the standard counterfactual definition, again, we must say no because if I had not pushed at all, your thumb would have been more than enough. My thumb did, however, happen to occupy a necessary slot; that is, some amount of force was necessary to push the button down, and I actually supplied part of that. Thus, for each of us, a portion of the pressure we applied was a cause of the machine's starting. The important point here is that in all cases of this sort, and there are many, something physical did occur, even if it is at the level of neurons or molecules and even if there is no way to know about it. In principle, the actual physical events paint the true causal scene. Precisely the same is true in the case of the student's own college, her parents' college, and income. Statistically, no cause emerges at all because income in these data was the same when the respondent did not go to college as when she did, and similarly for the parents' college. The fact is, however, that either the student's own college, her parents' college, or both were causal in each instance under the definition of factual cause (but not under the traditional definition), whether we can discern it at this moment or not. More detailed data on the manner of achieving the incomes, and a tracing of the physical causes and encounters in the chain, would presumably show this to be the case (but would not have the power of changing the incorrect inference under the traditional definition). This observation, in turn, is apparently of substantial importance for our central topic for it suggests that we must frequently probe more deeply than the revelations of the statistical analysis in order to discern the causal relations that underlie it. Can such probing actually reveal the causal relation when the dependent variable is some description of human behavior? I believe so, and each of the subsequent chapters will be devoted in part to substantiating the claim.

Alphonse and Gaston. "The fact that Gaston punctured the canteen (X) caused the fact that Henri died of thirst (Y)." X (puncturing) is a let-happen cause; if the water supply had been allowed to continue, Henri's critical water-processing functions would not have ground to a halt. Thus, being necessary in the counterfactual perspective as well as occupying a necessary slot in the physical causal scenario, Gaston's action was surely a cause. Essentially, however, the problem of redundancy that this case is supposed to present has cleverly and in fact arbitrarily been evaded by stipulating "died of thirst" instead of something equally descriptive but causally more problematic. What if, for example, we took for Y the fact that Henri died young or died while crossing the desert?

If we take this view of the fact in need of causal explanation, then the necessary condition perspective fails, but the revised version does not. We note that Gaston's action was not a standard necessary condition for the death at this specified time because Alphonse's poison would have taken over if Gaston had not punctured the canteen. Thus, the counterfactual definition fails. We intuitively see that it was indeed Gaston's action that led to Henri's death at this time, even if he would have died anyway, but we are prevented by the definition from calling his action a cause of any sort. Lewis's counterfactual chain solution also fails: Ostensibly, if Gaston had not punctured the canteen (not X), Henri would not have become parched (not Z), and if he had not become parched (which cleverly shifts the death back to a death by thirst), he would not have died in the desert (not Y), so Gaston is a cause. But are we sure of this second stage? We are impelled to ask why he would not have become parched, and there are a great many possibilities with a variety of causal implications. Perhaps he did not become parched because Gaston never punctured the canteen, as in the first stage counterfactual, in which case Henri would have been poisoned and Gaston is *not* guilty. Or, if our hypothetical "not becoming parched" is tied to a caravan's or a rainstorm's coming along so that he drank safe rather than poisoned water (Katz 1987)—as Lewis would no doubt prefer—then the counterfactual chain makes Gaston guilty again. Because we feel compelled to view many possibilities, it is *uncer-*

tain how Henri would have died or been saved in case he hypothetically had not become parched, and the counterfactual argument fails.

The revised definition does not fail, however, because, by being a let-happen cause of the actual, physical death, Gaston's action did occupy a necessary slot in the physical causal scenario. Physical causation here allows us—indeed compels us—to recognize and specify further that the death happened to be a death by thirst, even while the formal description of it is merely as a death while crossing the desert. Alphonse's action of poisoning, of course, did not occupy a necessary slot of any kind, since Henri died of thirst.

Collateral Effects. We are naturally expert in dealing with collateral effects; managing them in causal terms is second nature. This is so because so very many events have more than one effect. It rained (*W*), you stayed indoors (*X*), and the garden grew (*Y*). We all know that the garden did not grow because you stayed indoors, even though had you not stayed indoors it would not have rained and the garden would not have grown. The true reason why, for ordinary mortals, we do not make causes out of collateral effects is that it never occurs to us that *X* in these circumstances was a necessary condition for *Y*. What is our thinking if that idea is thrust upon us?

Consider James and John again. The problem emanates from the idea that if James had not been pleased, then, given all of the laws of nature and the actual circumstances of the case, the Tories must not have won the election and John would not have been sad. Mackie (1980: 33–34) suggests the possible solution of operating in terms of a hypothetical world that differs from the actual world as follows: The Tories won and everything else happened exactly as it did up until the time for James to be pleased, when instead he turns out not to have been pleased. In this way, James was not pleased but John was sad anyway, so that James was not a cause. Mackie notes, however, that realistically and deterministically speaking, James's not being pleased must somehow involve a violation of what were taken to be "the circumstances" (given the circumstances, if the Tories won it was impossible for James not to have been pleased). Lewis (1973) points out that James's not being pleased necessitates a violation of *something* and that violating the circumstances along the lines suggested by Mackie (e.g., James's newspaper was late, whereas John's was on time) is *less* of a violation than supposing that the Tories never won.

That sort of solution to the problem of collateral effects might withstand some challenges, but it would be vulnerable to the concoction of an example in which the worst violation were somehow a violation of the later circumstances rather than the original cause. For example, he made the whole throwing motion (W), the ball flew (X), and he winced from the pain in his shoulder (Y). The ball flew because he threw it. If the ball did not fly, presumably he simply did not make the whole throwing motion, so that the flying thereby unreasonably becomes the cause of the wincing. It is difficult to think what minor violation of the circumstances might have kept the ball from flying even though he made the whole throwing motion.

This process of picking and choosing among the factors that are to be considered responsible for the counterfactual condition on X suggests quite properly that we should, at this point, apply the argument from Annie, Manny, and the secretary of state, to wit: The *original* challenge of collateral effects to the counterfactual definition is no challenge at all. It cannot be said that if James had not been pleased John would not have been sad but only that he *might* not have been sad, depending on *why* James is imagined not to have been pleased, and that is not enough to make James a cause by the counterfactual definition. The reply seems valid initially (in fact it is not), but to me it is an evasion of the principle under which the problem of collateral effects does present a challenge. It is a challenge because it points out to us that we *can* have a necessary condition that was not a cause, so that the counterfactual definition only fairly successfully emulates but does not truly grasp our intuitive notion of causation.

Note that any successful response to the challenge of collateral effects depends on the possibility of the conjunction of W with not X; that is, in order to escape the conclusion that James was a cause, the Tories *must* be able to have won *without* James's being pleased. Of course, such combinations of W with not X because of late newspapers and so forth may be possible, but see what a ridiculous position we have gotten into by making them critical. If in the circumstances James's not being pleased somehow *entailed* that the Tories did not win, for example—and note that this is merely staying with our original formulation that W *was sufficient in the strong sense*—then we would be forced to accept that James's being pleased was the cause of John's being sad. The counterfactual definition must therefore identify X as a cause whenever W was sufficient in the strong sense, and that is absurd.

The way we naturally think about this kind of situation is completely different. If James had not been pleased, we can freely admit the possibility that W was sufficient in the strong sense, so that the Tories must not have won; we do not have to shut this out at all costs. Why? Because if the Tories were imagined in that case not to have won, so that John would not have been sad, it would still never occur to us to think that his actual sadness was caused by James's being pleased. We would simply and readily presume that two separate people did or did not get into certain emotional states because the potential cause of both of those states (*known by another definition*) did or did not materialize. As noted previously, our naive opinion of the case is that James was not the cause. In fact, we *know* that James was not the cause, in spite of all of the counterfactual reasoning, because it is plain that he had nothing in the world to do with John's being sad; that is, there was no physical causal flow of any sort going from James to John.

The revised definition of factual cause is built on this kind of reasoning because it starts with a definition of physical causality rather than depending on counterfactuals to supply the entire notion of cause. In this case, although in the classic sense X might be considered necessary for Y, it does not occupy a slot that was necessary for Y in the physical causal scenario. What does X (James's being pleased) or the slot it occupies (James's being anything or anybody's being pleased) have to do with the physical causal flow from the election to John's emotions? It is only an element at the end of *another* causal chain emanating from the election. Nor are James's emotions a let-happen cause. Unlike the case of the shutter or the 70-mph speed limit, we could switch James's being pleased on and off, and in fact we could switch James on and off altogether without its having the slightest impact on the effect of the election on John. Thus, we may *allow* that if the Mackie-Lewis rescue attempt were settled, it might well be settled against them, that is, in such a way as to force us to accept James's being pleased as a necessary condition for John's being sad. But even so we would not allow it as a cause. It fails to have a proper role in the focal instance of physical causation.

The example of James and John seems far from social science research, but the problem they represent is not. Collateral effects can be a serious threat to valid causal inference in case studies and, as noted previously, constitute the single-instance version of spurious causation, which is a similarly severe problem for many large- and small-n research designs. The nature of that problem to the researcher is getting at true causes in part by recognizing the spurious ones for what they are. As previously reviewed, the counterfactual definition forces us to consider spurious causes as true causes, but we do not and certainly do not want to think of them in that way. Consider, for example, the prominent case of indicators chosen because they are effects of concepts not directly measurable (or at least not measured), as the GRE score (X), for example, is supposedly an indicator of certain intellectual abilities (W). If we view results showing a strong relationship between GRE scores and performance in graduate school (Y), it would not occur to us to consider the GRE scores a cause. Furthermore, if we accept that low GRE scores to some extent truly do reflect meager ability (i.e., if not X then not W—the implication that the Mackie-Lewis maneuver tries to avoid), which is the whole point of using the test as an indicator, it still would not occur to us to conclude, on that account, that the GRE scores must themselves be a cause of the graduate school performance. It is factual causality, with its fundamentally physical component, that reflects the way in which we naturally think about such issues and that obviates the challenge of collateral effects.

Make-happen and Let-happen Causes. It was shown to be a flaw of the counterfactual definition that it does not recognize the distinction between make-happen and let-happen causes, a distinction that we readily and frequently make in practice. On the other hand, the dual conceptualization does permit the distinction and indeed promotes it to a central conceptual status. Factual causation is in one sense superordinate because any physical cause will also fit the definition of factual causation (the reverse is not true). In a more important sense, however, "make happen," which refers to physical causation, is the critical concept because it underlies and makes rigorous the rich and highly varied vocabulary connected with factual causation (let-happen causes, nonoccurrences, encounters, and so forth). If reasons, decisions, or choices are causes under the dual conceptualization, then they are probably *physical* as well as factual causes. If somehow they are to be factual causes only, then in order to reach the determination that they are at least causes in that sense we would feel the need to understand the scenario, that is, understand their relation to the factors that *are* the make-happen causes—the ones that exercise the kind of direct control over behavior that most concerns us.

Multiple Causation. It has often been pointed out to me that the counterfactual definition makes so many things into causes of Y as to be pragmatically awkward. It is perhaps true that William Marshal would not have entered the tournament if he had not wanted to confirm his loyalty to the English king (see Duby 1985), but it is also true that he would not have entered if he had not gotten out of bed that morning and if he had not at some point learned how to ride a horse. It would, in short, be more convenient if the definition of causality carried *in itself* the instructions for limiting an immense profusion of causes down to the one, or even the few, that are important. In the case of factual causality, however, just as with the standard counterfactual analysis, causes are multiple and the "importance" of causes is a matter of personal or social perspective.

The problem is that in many situations there are several factors or combinations of factors that might be considered to be the critical cause. The final determination, regardless of what philosophers or social scientists might advise, will depend on such things as social norms, morality, and power. We would usually ignore getting up in the morning as a cause of some disaster, for example, because our norms suggest that one should not be held responsible for any unusual and unpredictable results of doing what is normal and expected. Similarly, either the ball or the shutter might become more important in assigning responsibility for the broken window if, for example, Mrs. Jones had told Johnny not to play ball around the house and he defied this recognized authority or she had told Jimmy not to open the shutter when the kids were playing ball and he ignored the clear and present danger about which he had been warned. One might either try to build such rules into the definition of factual causation itself or leave causation simple, allow multiple causes, and recognize that their pertinence to social theory and to applied social science must be established by additional and indeed mutable criteria. It seems to me far better to opt for the latter approach. (See Smiley 1991 for a discussion of the social determination of moral responsibility in just this connection.)

Begging the Question. This has been a severe, and by its very nature a largely unrecognized, problem in most discourse regarding causality (cf. Davidson 1980: 76–81). We ran into it in the counterfactual definition in the context of the inevitable appeal to "other causes" of Y and will find it cropping up again in subsequent chapters. The reason for this tendency toward circular definition, I suggest, is that a natural, ingrained, and mostly automatic and subconscious way of thinking about causation in the everyday life that formed all of us is in terms of physical links, but we have been denied access to that tool in scholarly treatments of causation. When we beg the question, betraying that we know something is or is not causal even though we cannot establish that fact by the various strained definitions we are trying to justify, it is physical causation that gives us our backdoor view.

We have found other roles for physical causation as well, in particular the role of the conception against which we test the adequacy of the counterfactual definition in various cases. In the present chapter, we have operated without demonstration as though these claims about the role of physical causality were valid, doing so in order to grapple first with the theory of causation that is most prominent at present in social science—the counterfactual view. In the next chapter, I will therefore define and defend the idea of physical causation so that it may be seen as playing with validity the roles I have already suggested for it as well as serving as a basis for the further methodological inquiry to be pursued in the chapters that follow.

Chapter 2

Physical Cause

In work on the theory of causation, three proposals are intimately connected with the idea of physical cause—physical causation itself as proposed here, the regularity theory, and the manipulability theory. We begin with a very brief consideration of the last of these.

The Manipulability Theory

Of the many proposals for a definition of causation that have been offered (see Beauchamp 1974; Sosa 1975; Brand 1976), many of which are more appropriate to philosophical than social-science kinds of treatment, the manipulability theory requires review in this context both because it incorporates a variant of physical causation and because it apparently taps a common notion of the derivation of the idea of cause (Collingwood 1940; Gasking 1974; von Wright 1971).

The idea is that people know about causation because they have the experience of doing certain things and seeing other things result. People can strike a thin, sturdy piece of metal and find that it results in the sound "Gong!" The harder they strike it, the louder it sounds. From countless experiences such as this, we are told, our idea of causation emerges. Thus, X was a cause of Y when by manipulating X we could have brought Y about. It is true that there are many things we cannot manipulate but that we nevertheless consider to be causes. For example, we might find that the darkness caused Annie to stumble, but it is not as though we could manipulate the darkness. On second thought, however, we might. We do not necessarily have to bring around the sun but might switch a bank of floodlights on and off, let us say. In short, there are ways in which we can imagine accomplishing much the same thing as almost any event that occurs in nature.

The manipulability theory has general value because it suggests that the concept of causation arises out of our own physical experience, and therefore it encourages us to look closely at that experience before accepting the impossibility of finding causality "in the objects." We will do so momentarily.

The manipulability theory, however, does have its defects. It might seem at first glance to overcome the problem of collateral effects since we could not bring about John's being sad just by manipulating James's being pleased. James, then, is properly found by the manipulability theory not to be a cause. Unfortunately, however, we have achieved this victory by begging the question, a perennial trap in discussions of the definition of cause (Sosa 1975: 7; Brand 1976: 28–30). Seeing other things "result," "manipulating" X, and "bringing about" Y are all locutions that depend on a prior or external conceptualization of causality. They cannot themselves be interpreted in terms of the manipulability theory without making the definition hopelessly circular. Again, the suggestion is clear that the underlying notion of causation taken for granted is ordinary physical cause.

One might try to salvage the situation by changing the definition in the following way in order to avoid terms such as "result": "if we had done X, then Y would have *occurred*." But then we open up the floodgates for the concerns familiar from the critique of the counterfactual definition, such as coincidence, collateral effects, and redundancy (Sosa 1975: 7; Brand 1976: 28–30). If a person did his or her deep-breathing exercises every morning just before sunrise, for example, then this definition would make the deep-breathing exercises the cause of the sunrise. Or, if Senator Jones always advocated and voted for the position favored by the most powerful senator on the committee, and the committee always ratified this position, then Senator Jones must necessarily be a cause of the committee's choice. And lastly, because Fannie's yelling "Look out!" is followed by the proper corrective action both in general and in this instance, then Fannie must be the cause of Annie's jumping even when Manny has drowned her out.

The manipulability theory has intuitive appeal, but question-begging once more shows that, in itself, it is neither what we mean by causation nor how we know about it.

Physical Cause and the Humean View

Because of Hume, the possibility of physical causation is so intertwined with the regularity theory that we will consider both together, beginning with a brief documentation of the Humean analysis of causality.

Having given up on being able to find causation "in the objects," Hume located it in *regularity,* or "constant conjunction," and also in an associational propensity of the mind. He defines cause as "an object followed by another, and where all the objects, similar to the first, are followed by objects similar to the second" and a few lines later as "an object followed by another, and whose appearance always conveys the thought to that other" (Hume 1955: 84–89). In other words, one sort of event causes another when it is always *followed by* the other and in such a way as to lead people to expect the sequence automatically. In more recent times, the neo-Humean doctrine is that our knowledge of causality and our sense of the meaning of the term inhere in universal laws.

It is possible that Hume's problem in failing to find causality in the singular instance was that his consideration was dominated by the sense of vision even though he did consider another tack that in my view was more promising (Farrer 1960: 184). Following the observation of Strawson (1985: 123), who cites Farrer (1960), I suggest that the animal senses involved in *feeling* are a much better source. We may have the idea of causation, in other words, because in certain instances we can feel our bodies being buffeted or strained, and this seems to be a kind of experience shared universally among human beings. Accordingly, I will offer a definition of physical causality that rests on the ability of certain parts of the body to feel what are interpreted as forces and motion. In doing so, I will abide by empiricist constraints but will take a different tack from Hume's in solving the central problem, namely, the problem of how we are able to derive an idea of a *relation* between objects, which is an abstraction, by observing something *empirically* in the real world. Assuming that all of us have a rough, intuitive sense of the law of inertia, the sort of motion to which I will refer in this context is an inertial diversion, that is, motion of a hand, shoulder, and the like, that is a diversion from what would otherwise have been its inertial path. I offer a basic definition that involves the body alone and then augment it with a more general definition, pertaining to all objects, obtained by projection.

The Definition

At a minimum, physical causation is a relation between a force exerted on a feeling part of the body and a motion of the same part, the force and the motion being felt as such and being associated with one another by virtue of the sensation of a transfer of momentum. The force then gives rise to the idea of "cause" and the motion to the idea of "effect."

It is not necessary and perhaps not possible to detail the basis of the sensation of transfer of momentum, where the proposed solution to the central problem resides, but one may note at least the likely role of a sense of matching of the force and motion in terms of location, time, direction, and strength. The elements within us that are responsible for the sensation when it occurs are at the level of cells and their linkages. It is clear, however, (*a*) that the body is *not* equipped to feel the general macroevent as the real collection of distinct molecular and electrical happenings that make it up and (*b*) that the body *is* equipped to interpret the entire microset simultaneously as one single happening that links the force and the motion together (cf. "continuity" and "persistence" in Mackie 1980: 142, 217–30).

If this were all there was to physical causation, then it would involve our own bodies alone. We find, however, that the same sort of relation exists between billiard balls, stones and windows, and so forth. Knowing about this extension is purely a psychological projection (therefore far more prone to error) by which we mentally substitute the body for external objects of all sorts that are seen, read about, or otherwise experienced. Essentially, if we see a billiard ball being hit on the table, we say quite automatically, "If that billiard ball were my head, I would feel it in such and such a way." In actuality, we never know whether we are right about this or not, that is, whether or not we actually would feel it in that way. If we are correct, it is physical causation that is taking place out there. If we are incorrect, it is not. In referring to substituting the body for "external" objects, I mean external to the feeling parts of the body as stipulated in the definition, but such objects to which we must project very definitely and importantly include parts of the body as well—the nonfeeling parts, such as neurons, molecules of tissue, blood cells, and so forth.

Thus, to repeat the above at the general level: Physical causation is a relation between a force on an object and a motion of the same object, such that if the object were a feeling part of the body, the pair would be felt to be force and motion, respectively, and would be associated with one another by virtue of the sensation of a transfer of momentum. When a feeling part of the body is itself the object, the force then gives rise to the idea of "cause" and the motion to the idea of "effect."

This *feeling* of the force as separate from the motion it produces comes about in the following way: Consider, for example, that I see one billiard ball strike another on the table and witness the second ball's scooting away. The effect I attribute to the force carried by the first ball is the motion of the second one. Similarly, say that I watch as someone shoves your shoulder and your shoulder lurches backward. The effect of the shove, I would say, is the backward motion of your shoulder and upper body. Now say that it were *my* shoulder that was shoved. I not only *feel* the very same effect in the form of a motion that, when it was your shoulder, I only saw, but I also feel the force of the shove itself, over and above that, because of the impression it makes on the nerves in my skin and the tissue beneath the skin and the capacity of my body to translate those impressions into a sense of touch and pressure. In point of fact, the same things were happening when it was your shoulder that was being shoved, but I could not know that. All I was aware of was the gross motion of your shoulder, *and if that external causation were the only sort I ever experienced, it is problematic whether I would ever have the idea of causation at all.* Hume's "followed by" version is a possible source, of course, but we will see that this source is fraught with so much confusion that it is an unlikely basis for the clear idea of causation that we have. As it is, my body provides me with an additional experience of the event in each single personal instance beyond what I perceive when the same event is external, and it is this added dimension that gives me more insight into causation than regularity would alone. Observing the billiard balls naively, I see only two motions, but projecting from bodily experience I clearly perceive a motion and a force. If a gust of wind stops me in my tracks, I can feel the force of the wind on my face and body, and I can also feel the inertial diversion in the effort it takes to work against the force—a degree of effort that otherwise would be coupled with my moving along much more rapidly. To take another example, it would be hard to convince me that people were not just joking and pretending to strain if I naively observed them trying to push two strong magnets together because I *see* nothing in between but space. But when I finally do it for myself, I can *feel*, and thereafter project, that the force is there, just as though it were housed in a strong, visible spring.

Thus, our knowledge of cause and effect comes always from dividing into two segments the events specified in the definition when a force is felt by certain parts of the body. Some of the events we interpret as the motion associated with the force and some as the identity of the force itself. It is the former events—the set of associated motions—that we categorize in light of the sensation of transfer of momentum to be a physical effect. The other events—the feeling of the wind on our faces, the hurt of the blow to the shoulder, the effort of pushing the two magnets together—these are how we know that the force is there.

We see at the same time that physical causation as directly experienced operates at the gross or aggregate level, the level of whole, feeling objects and not parts or particles. By projection, the effect of one billiard ball's striking another is generally taken to be the motion of the second ball as a whole and not the unseen motion of individual molecules adjacent to the point of impact. To be able to think of causation in relation to a molecule, we must shift focus to one of those molecules itself as a whole object and forget about the ball.

The question may arise whether the force-identifying feeling of which we speak is not itself an effect in an instance of physical causation given that the force that causes the shoulder to move is also the cause of that feeling. If it is an effect, then in order to satisfy the definition (viz., when there is an effect, the force that produced it can be independently identified) there must be some *additional* way of discerning the existence of the force. But we have run out; we have no *additional* feeling of the force that is causing the feeling but just the one feeling by itself, the one that is in this new light being considered an effect. This apparent problem is clarified, as suggested above, by recognizing that the motion involved in feeling what is now proposed to be an effect here is not a motion of a feeling part of the body as required by the definition. The motions involved are at the level of cells, neurons, electrons, neurotransmitters, and so forth. In other words, the feeling of a force that identifies it as such is indeed an instance of physical causation but of the projected variety, not the directly perceived. It is comparable to the motion of individual molecules around the site of impact in the second billiard ball. We cannot feel the force that produces the motion in such molecules or cells but can only project that such a feeling would be there if such a molecule were our shoulder or our head.

In these ways, rightly or wrongly, our bodies give us the idea that there are physical forces and a sense of a particular kind of connectedness between things that goes beyond "followed by"—a kind of connectedness that we come to label causation. If our bodies are not misleading us, then we have here at least a hint about physical causation as it actually exists in nature, namely, that it inheres partly in a force. The hint is only a crude one because the natures of the forces are not clear to us. Apparently, our bodies will never make this clear on their own. We delegate the task of developing an understanding of forces to the physicists.

Hume on Feeling

Although the notion that knowledge of causation arises in this way has not been much discussed in philosophy, it is not new. As pointed out both by Strawson (1985: 123) and Mackie (1980: 24), the possible role of feeling was noted by Hume himself. In considering how we know causation and distinguish it from noncausal events, Hume wrote in a footnote: "No animal can put external bodies in motion without the sentiment of a *nisus* [effort] or endeavor; and every animal has a sentiment or feeling from the stroke or blow of an external object that is in motion" (1955: 88). However, Hume dismisses this source of knowledge, and with it the whole notion of knowledge of causation as a force or power: "These sensations," he says, "are merely animal," and from them, "we can *a priori* draw no inference." Their existence "is no proof that we are acquainted, in any instance, with the connecting principle between cause and effect." Hume's concern is that we do not understand the nature of the power that is ostensibly involved because we do not experience a connection between two events but rather just a single event, which some would say we interpret as indicating a "force." Aside from the question of whether Hume is correct in this observation, we may at least notice in the passage that there is apparently a certain descriptive accuracy to the proposition that we do make an inferential leap from feelings to forces.

The taking of this leap as a common experience did not go unnoticed by Hume. As he elaborated in another footnote: "It may be pretended, that the resistance which we meet with in bodies, obliging us frequently to exert our force and call up all our power, this gives us the idea of force and power. It is this *nisus* or strong endeavor of which we are conscious, that is the original impression from which this idea is copied" (1955: 78–79). The word *pretended* is used in the first of these sentences because of Hume's insistence that we cannot rely upon such feelings of "force" to give us an accurate idea of a *causal* power. Nevertheless, he accepts that there is a general tendency to make the inference and that the tendency should not be overlooked: "It must, however, be confessed that the animal *nisus* which we experience, though it can afford no accurate precise idea of power, enters very much into that vulgar, inaccurate idea which is formed of it" (1955: 79). We can now remark that the feeling of an effort or a blow by itself is indeed not enough because the particular effects of the force that produce the feeling—the motions involving neurons and other cells—are not, to us, the motions of sensory objects. But the feeling of the force coupled with the sense of an accompanying motion of a feeling part of the body and joined by the feeling of a transfer of momentum between the two is enough, and these elements, indeed, comprise the set that underlies all knowledge of causation.

I suggest that the approach to causation through physical feelings, given that it underpins the definition of factual causation as well as standing alone as a conceptualization, accounts for all or nearly all ordinary causal language. The theory is mirrored in practice in other ways, too. For example, there should be more doubt about causation among external objects than causation involving feeling parts of the body, and that tendency apparently does exist. Similarly, there should be and actually is more doubt about causal occurrences among molecules and particles than among objects than can be seen or felt. How flame and heat come about, for example, remains fairly mysterious to most of us. Even though they are part of regular experience, the role of causation in their production remains quite obscure. The same is true of the physiological generation of intentional human behavior: we take on faith that there must be some causation involved somehow, although we do not know quite what we refer to as "cause" when we use it in this connection. Last, the causal role of gravity is again an article of faith. Its manner of working cannot yet be imagined even by projection.

Physical Causation and Regularity

Hume chose the regularity theory, whereas I have opted here for physical causation. One would think, however, that there must be an intimate relation between the two because if X is the physical cause of Y in one instance it must be so in all instances under the same conditions, so that physical causation is simply another way of arriving at the regularity theory. Moreover, the proper orientation for social science should therefore be—as it has widely been, especially in quantitative social science—to seek systematic generalizations concerning human behavior and its causes. I want to suggest (*a*) that the regularity theory is unsatisfactory as a conceptualization of causality for social science, (*b*) that it is in fact unsatisfactory altogether, and (*c*) that although there is a strong empirical connection between physical causation and regularity, the two are conceptually distinct in critical ways.

If there are general laws of human behavior, then they connect certain causes with human behaviors as effects. To anticipate the next chapter somewhat, it is clear that the most prominent candidates for this general causal role in social science are mental events of a certain kind. We will see that *reasons* represent the primary contender, but others that have merited consideration are desires, intentions, motives, decisions, acts of will or choice, and so on. Thus, if causation is properly rendered by the regularity theory in social science, and if reasons, desires, and so forth are causes, then there must apparently be laws connecting these entities with behavior. Here is where, in the Humean perspective, social science is in trouble. If the way in which we know about the causation of human behavior is to observe an object such as a reason, followed by another such as a behavior, and where all the objects similar to the first are followed by objects similar to the second, then we apparently know of no causation in the human sciences.

Perhaps the laws are operative, but, due to the complexity of human affairs, we cannot readily make such observations. I will briefly suggest here, and provide a demonstration in chapter 3, that such is not the case—that there can indeed be no such laws.

Intuitively, there is sound even if not conclusive reason to believe initially that no law can exist connecting reasons as a class with behavior as a class (there would be such a law if whenever there were a reason of any sort the corresponding action would follow, and vice versa). It seems that we often perform intentional behaviors without any conscious reasons at all ("I realized that I was scolding the little fellow for an innocent act but could think of no reason why I would do so") and frequently have active reasons that are never acted upon. Many of us are motivated to visit the birthplaces of our parents in the old country, but not all of us do so in spite of having both the active reason and the capability to carry it out.

Nor does there appear to be a lawlike connection between *specific* behaviors and *specific* reasons or desires, such as innovative behavior's being universally explained by the desire for prestige, war by the desire for expansion or domestic security, or voter turnout by the desire to do one's duty as a citizen, and so on. Nor will it help matters to string any number of such desires or reasons together for we must allow that there have been or might always arise some people who simply would not perform the behavior even though they had that particular string of reasons. Nor will it help to stipulate that such reasons predict universally but only under certain conditions for as soon as the conditions are specified precisely it becomes clear that, even then, there might be individuals somewhere, at some time, who do not or would not go to war or adopt an innovation even if they had those reasons and the specified conditions were also fulfilled (Dray 1957: 31–37). There is always the possibility of an exceptional further reason or condition. Some perhaps believe that laws connecting specific reasons with specific behaviors may yet be discovered, but we may at least observe at this point that several centuries of social science have not yet allowed us to import causality into the disciplines by that particular route.

Of course, one might trivialize. Knowing that there were only two people in the room who felt uncomfortably warm and that both loosened their ties on that account, one might declare the universal causal law that everyone in room R at time t (already past) who wants relief from the heat will loosen his or her tie by time $t + 5$. It is in fact not easy to be certain whether such trivializations must be counted as universal laws, but it seems probable that, in any case, they can never be part of social science and therefore cannot relieve our anxiety by establishing causality on a firm foundation within the discipline. As a science, quantitative or qualitative, we need generalizations that teach and are intriguing and are falsifiable and that form a basis for prediction and social control—that are anything, in short, but trivial.

In sum, it is at least questionable whether we can generate systematic generalizations about intentional behavior. If we do a historical, cultural, structural, or psychological analysis and suggest that the causes of an observed behavior were certain desires, attitudes, or ambitions or certain environmental, political, economic, or social-structural conditions, there is an excellent chance that, under the regularity theory, the term *cause* would be applied illegitimately since there would probably be no valid way to connect the relation found to any true universal. Most of us, however, would feel that causation of some sort had indeed taken place in these instances.

One response of great importance to this predicament is to assert that behavior is physical and that it therefore *must* be governed by laws.

And if it is in any sense governed by laws, then somehow there are legitimate physical notions that validate our social science explanations (that is, the ones that are correct). But this assumption is not justified; it should give no comfort. Just because something is physical, and therefore is subject to the laws of physics, does not mean that there are laws governing that something as we describe it or classify it. For example, the wearing of rocks (as by wind and rain) and the movement of sand and dunes are physical and are subject to the laws of physics, but there are no laws governing the wearing of rocks or the movement of sand per se (see Davidson on hurricanes [1980, 17]). It is hard to see how we can learn *from regularities* that these events are the effects of causes, which they surely are, when they are not subject to regularities of any sort. Is human behavior similar in this way to the movement of sand? I will argue that it is.

In this circumstance, it is natural to question the general soundness of the regularity theory of causation. Before reviewing some of the difficulties, let me try to insist polemically that the regularity theory is not right because we all know that it is wrong. When one billiard ball hits another one on the table, we do not identify the resulting movement of the balls as causal because of a "followed by" rule or a turn of the mind. We do so because we see that some common, overwhelmingly evident physical thing has happened between two entities, whether we know how to identify it satisfactorily in the objects or not.

More to the point of the analysis of causality, the regularity theory has disappointed because it has proven vexingly difficult to find a principle that distinguishes a "true" universal, reflecting a causal law, from various other types of universal relation such as coincidences, social rules or norms, spurious causation, experience due to change in position (as daytime following night), developmental sequences (as the tree following the planting of the acorn), and classificatory characteristics (as in "all swans are white"). To illustrate just briefly, consider the two individuals above who were uncomfortably warm, but now change the story so that, instead of loosening their ties, we observe that each wrote a note in his pocketbook—by coincidence, as it happens, but we can only observe regularity, not cause versus coincidence. We can then declare the universal law that every time somebody feels warm in room R at time t (specified to be, say, 1:00 PM last November 16), he writes a note in his pocketbook by time $t + 5$. Thereby, we deduce that warmth under those conditions causes one to write in one's pocketbook. Similarly, we would have a law stipulating that all presidents of the United States in the nineteenth (and twentieth?) centuries are male.

Or consider the relationship between attending college and political participation. Admittedly, it is not universal, but some anyway might assume that it is universal under certain conditions and that eventually, with further study, we would hope to unearth those conditions. If it is a universal relation, it must therefore be causal. But this is unsatisfactory because the two might very well be spuriously related, at least in part. That is, it is possible that a third factor, family background perhaps, independently causes both college attendance and political participation, at least to some extent. Nor does it help matters in the case of spuriousness to stipulate that the universal relation between X and Y is causal only to the extent that there is no third factor that is universally related to both since this will hopelessly confound sources of spuriousness with intervening links that transmit true causation. For example, if attending college actually were at least a partial cause of greater political participation, then "the feeling that my participation would be efficacious" might be such an intervening link: attending college causes the feeling of efficacy and the feeling of efficacy causes political participation. Now that we have found a third factor that is universally related to both of the first two, however, our modified rule would require us to eliminate college attendance totally as a cause of participation. We would not want the discovery of intervening links transmitting causation, which almost always exist, to force us to categorize true causal relationships as noncausal. Nor, finally, would it help to try to save transmitted causation and still get rid of spuriousness in the definition by specifying that there be no *temporally prior* third factor that is universally related to both. Under this rule, we see that the first cause in a chain (such as attending college) is such a temporally prior third factor, so that now the intervening link (such as a feeling of efficacy) could not be counted as causal.

Thus, to say that regularity plays the role of the source of the idea of causation is, I would claim, far-fetched in the extreme for only with the aid of science, statistics, and modern philosophy can we have a clear enough idea of what must be intended by the ambiguous, cumbersome, and altogether elusive concept of regularity to come anywhere close to being able to use it as a source of knowledge about causation—and even then the effort fails. In Hume's philosophy, for example, the idea of causation derives from an "impression" that is a habit of mind—the expectation of Y that we experience when we see X occur, having seen Y follow X numerous times in the past, as in the collision of billiard balls on the table (Hume 1955: 86, 89). This solution to the central philosophical problem is of course tenuous. The "sensory" impression that amounts to an expectation of Y upon observing X is not related to the regular observation of X and Y in just the same way as the sensory impression of a chair is related to a chair. But this is to be expected: it cannot be straightforward to get an empiricist account of a relation as opposed to an object. What is far more troublesome is that the account offered implies that we should be able to derive the idea of causation from regularities such as those just reviewed—from the expectation that the day will follow the night and from spurious relations, and so forth. But if we derived an idea of causation in part from our expectation that these Ys would follow upon these Xs, and if we then felt the need to reconcile these various relations with one another and with the clash of billiard balls on a table as being all of the same type, then such an idea of causation could only be either muddled, grotesque, or vacuous. I suggest that we know about causation from the other source, from feeling, and that *we in fact use this knowledge to test whether such experienced regularities are causal regularities or not*, for otherwise we would be quite confused. In the case of these patterns brought up to challenge the regularity theory, of course, (spurious effects, day and night, warmth and pocketbooks, etc.) we reject the notion since projection from our bodily experience with forces and motion leads us to classify each of them as noncausal rather than causal. None is the same sort of thing as our physical causal experience at all.

Thus, the unfortunate consequences of hewing to an empiricism that will not admit forces on the basis of feelings are the monumental difficulties that follow from resorting to regularity in the theory of causes (Ducasse 1966; Mackie 1980: 3–4; Beauchamp 1974: 74–114). Beyond the confounding variety of regularities, however, there is legitimate cause for reservation in a difficulty that is not merely technical. It appears to me that the regularity theory has constricted the concept of causation considerably and choked off a good deal of its potential for constructive use. The regularity theory plays no constructive role whatever, for example, in enlightening the process of social research, so that we pay dearly for the traditional solution to the empiricist's problem. If we in social science depended fully on the regularity theory, we would never be able to say that some reason or norm or economic condition caused some particular behavior in the single instance, that is, in some particular observed individual or group. The solution in terms of physical causation, on the other hand, because of its connection to the causes of intentional behavior and the support and enrichment it offers to the counterfactual view, should be liberating. It should permit a genuine fertility instead of a constriction—a fertility that is more appropriate to and more to be expected from so fundamental an idea as that of causation.

In sum, although the regularity theory has not been totally abandoned, one knows that it has serious problems. And in any case social science would be more comfortable with a definition that depends on what happens in each single instance rather than on universal laws, given the tenuousness of the idea of universal laws in our disciplines.

We may ask, "Just how much of a departure from the regularity theory is involved in the move to physical causation, and what is the relation between the two?" First, although not all regularities are causal, all instances of physical causation by the conceptualization offered here are regular; that is, they are instances of universal (or nearly universal) laws *when properly described in terms of force and motion.* This means that a physical cause as here defined will always meet the test of regularity theory, so that the two will then agree. It is just that additional relations apparently also meet the test of regularity theory and confound analysis because they are not instances of physical causation. As I suggested a moment ago, it is in fact physical causation that enables us to distinguish the noncausal regularities from the causal ones. The action of forces is regular. At the same time, if a billiard ball is glued down, it is no less a "billiard ball," but it will not act or react causally as other billiard balls do. In articulating *why* this and other possible modifications of the ball lead to differing sensory impressions of its behavior, thereby adding amendments and qualifications to the regularity involving billiard balls, it is immediately apparent that one gets further and further from a regularity about billiard balls per se and closer and closer to a regularity about forces. In the theory of causes, a billiard ball is not an elemental actor, but merely a "holder" of forces— different forces at different times. In fact, *there is no true, experienced reg-*

ularity about billiard balls or any other such object but only regularities about forces: namely, Newton's first and second laws of motion, of which each action of a billiard ball is a thoroughly individualized instance.

The proposed definition of physical causality operates at the level of the single instance. Knowledge of causation depends on no laws, no regularities. If I have a direct causal experience of this sort one time, such as having my shoulder shoved or bumping into a brick wall, it is clearly the experience of a relation between a force and a motion even though I have never seen or heard of such a thing before. Similarly, although physical causes are regular in an important sense, this definition does not entail that there must be general causal laws. To arrive at that point, one must bring to the discussion some additional premise such as the need for everything that is physical to be covered by the laws of physics in Western science. For example, accepting physical causality puts me under no obligation to hew to determinism—to believe that every diversion from inertia has a cause. If I accepted that inertial diversions happened spontaneously in the world, I might frequently be uncertain or mistaken about whether an instance of causation had taken place, but I would not change my notion of causation in the slightest. There would simply be caused and uncaused diversions. We recognize, some of us with a sense of relief, that *there may in fact be no truly universal associations in the world, but there is causality.* If physics comes to see everything as uncertain and probabilistic at bottom, causation still remains.

In our culture, however, it is clear that since Newton our understanding of causality is Newtonian. Before, it was unsystematic; now, it is disciplined. The definition of physical causality does not depend on Newton, but it fits Newton's laws and is elaborated and illuminated by the Newtonian model. By now, that model helps us to understand what we mean by the unschooled notion of cause and helps us greatly to determine cause by projection when we experience it. Newton's laws (and others) describe what we know as causation in the single instance and universalize it. This implies, for one, that causes are not capricious, isolated, spiritual, or mysterious. They are part of a natural system marked by a considerable amount of order and predictability. If X seems sometimes to be the cause of Y and sometimes not, there must be a perfectly good Newtonian explanation. For example, if reasons or will seem sometimes to cause the appropriate behavior and sometimes not, as they surely do, then there either is a good Newtonian sense in which they are always causes or they will be shown not to be causes at all. Causation is independent of regularity in principle but very strongly associated in practice.

Thus, given that physical causes must in principle be regular, we have an important criterion for examining whether certain kinds of events can qualify as physical causes of intentional human behavior.

Chapter 3

The Causes of
Intentional Behavior

Armed with an analysis of causation, we now shift to a consideration of
the process that generates intentional behavior with a view toward connecting the two in the plane of ordinary social research.

The idea is that the definition of causality should be able to guide
our thinking regarding the kinds of things that may qualify as causes in
the social sciences, thus helping to point the way toward certain conclusions regarding methods. Physical cause should occupy a prominent place in the inquiry, thus the nature of the pertinent physiological
mechanism will become particularly germane. A Humean "followed
by" conceptualization or even reliance on factual causality would not
be completely adequate because the interest in what *makes* behavior
happen—whether it is our conscious choices or some other force—is
likely to persist for many of us if the causal question is answered in any
way that does not respond explicitly to this issue. Our attention will be
concentrated initially on the psychological concepts mentioned frequently as primary candidates for the generic causes of behavior—reasons, decisions, and so forth. In light of the first two chapters, are any of
these indeed generic causes?

They may clearly appear to have been necessary conditions and to
have occupied a necessary slot, at least to some of us some of the time.
We may believe without a shadow of a doubt that, for example, if
William Marshal had not decided to enter the tournament, he would
not have entered the tournament. But that is not enough. We want to
know whether it was that decision which physically made William
Marshal enter for, if not, we must then immediately ask what *additional*
thing it could possibly have been that did make him enter? The important question at issue would therefore seem to be: are reasons, desires,
will, choices, decisions, or similar categories of event the *physical* causes
of behavior? We will see that most of these can be eliminated, so that

only one possibility remains, a possibility I will label "operative reasons." I argue that it is not possible to determine whether operative reasons are indeed causes, however, without matching them up with what is known of the physiological mechanism that produces intentional behavior. Otherwise, conclusions can only be speculative and methodological inquiry is likely to remain ambiguous. The questions of whether physical causes exist as well as psychological explanations, whether they are essentially the same thing, and, if not, how they then can be reconciled with one another both in the body and in social science research paradigms—these questions would leave many of us with a sense of insecure understanding as long as they remained untreated. I will therefore include in this chapter an account of how affect and the system that uses it figure in the production of behavior and how operative reasons relate to that physiological mechanism.

Thoughts as Causes

We will consider all of the kinds of events mentioned just above but chief among them will be "reasons." Consequently, we need a definition of the term. There is fair agreement on the formal meaning of this concept, perhaps the most rigorous of the definitions being Davidson's (1980: 3). An agent has a reason for performing action *A* when he or she has (*a*) a pro attitude (want, desire, favorable inclination, etc.) toward actions of a certain kind and (*b*) a belief that *A* is an action of that kind. William Marshal, for example, entered the tournament because he had a pro attitude toward actions that would confirm his loyalty to the English king and a belief that entering the tournament was an action of that kind. A reason, therefore, always has two components: a desire and a belief.

I maintain that much of the literature on the subject of reasons as causes has been remiss in not specifying routinely whether reasons as *thoughts* were under consideration, or reasons not in the form of thoughts, or both. Many of us readily accept that reasons, desires, and so forth can be held at the subconscious level as well as the conscious. We will see that whichever of these we treat makes a critical difference in the outcome of the inquiry. By the term *thoughts* in this context I will refer only to certain kinds of thoughts, that is, to the conscious forms of reasons, decisions, and the like. Such thoughts do not have to be whole sentences, nor even be in language at all. We will require only that they be at least some vague, stirring awareness in the general form of the particular psychological event treated (reason, decision, etc.).

We have a special interest in thoughts as causes because many of us are concerned with whether people are in control of their own behavior, and if an individual behaved only in terms of nonconscious reasons, we would be unlikely to characterize him or her as "in control." On the contrary, we would be likely to say something to the effect that "this woman is being pushed around by her subconscious." It is my observation that most people do feel that their behavior is controlled, or at least controllable, by conscious decisions and choices. Is that feeling justified or not? I will generally cover both the conscious and subconscious forms with terms such as reason, decision, and the like, but the need to distinguish between them will frequently arise, and the text will then make the distinction explicitly.

For clarity, we must also distinguish a "behavior" from an "action" and specify which one we will target primarily as the kind of effect to be explained. A behavior, first, is any motion or lack of motion, but we will confine ourselves for the most part to bodily movements that constitute *intentional* behavior. This term cannot be defined until we have considered several other ideas in some depth, but for now we can specify it loosely as a residual category; that is, intentional behavior is behavior that is not in such other categories as continuous/automatic (e.g., breathing), accidental (falling down), mechanically forced (being pushed or drugged), or reflex (sneezing).

An action is an interpreted version of a set of intentional behaviors, it being understood (*a*) that the interpretation is in terms of "doing something" by those behaviors and (*b*) that the interpreted version actually occurred (cf. Davidson 1980: 43–62). To say that William Marshal entered the tournament is to refer to a collection of bodily movements that did occur and that amount to the doing of a certain something that we interpret by means of the designation "entered the tournament."

As soon as we try to describe a behavior, even a behavior of the simplest kind, we inevitably interpret it and make an action out of it by applying cultural terms. It would therefore seem to make a good deal of sense to concentrate on the explanation of actions. Nevertheless, we know that we can *refer to* a behavior as it exists in its pure, natural state, even though we are completely unable to describe it as such. It does exist, independently of any interpretations. We can, for example, say that we are concerned with the set of pure behaviors that we interpret as the health department's adopting the innovation of school mental health clinics. This action, adopting the innovation, is in fact quite a convenient packaging of the pure behaviors we wish to consider: we are not really certain just exactly which total group of subbehaviors we are talking about, but that generally does not matter. As Davidson puts it (1980: 51): "If I tie my shoelaces, here is a description of my movements: I move my body in just the way required to tie my shoelaces." There was some set of pure behaviors that we feel can be packaged into the action "tying my shoelaces" or "adopting the innovation of school mental health clinics," and our interest centers on whether a reason, for example, was or was not the cause of the performance of that set.

An action as such cannot be the effect of a physical cause, as defined in the previous chapter, because that must be a natural event—the motion of an object—whereas an action is a set of events not in their pure, natural state but as interpreted by some person. The action does, however, refer to a set of pure behaviors. We will therefore simplify greatly by concentrating our inquiry on the causes of these behaviors alone.

Unlike desires, decisions, and the rest, reasons explain actions in the rational sense, so that it is natural to inquire whether these entities that *explain the action* also *cause the behaviors* that make it up. This is an important juxtaposition. It would be a great convenience in social research if correct explanations that were satisfactory in the rational sense of shedding the light of understanding on an action were also correct in the scientific sense of reflecting true cause and effect in the empirical world. Correct historical explanations, for example, would then be scientific explanations by the causal criterion. There is one strong sense in which we betray in ordinary usage that reasons *are* considered causes, although this is not necessarily confined to reasons as thoughts. Consider it in the following terms: A reason provides a rational explanation in *form*; that is, if we think of the action "entering the tournament" as being William Marshal's practical conclusion about what to do, then the premises that led to the conclusion should be of such a form as to show (*a*) what he wanted to accomplish by such an act and (*b*) why he considered that this act would accomplish it. A reason for Marshal's entering the tournament, such as "William Marshal wanted to increase the probability of victory for the English knights and felt that only by entering himself would they be strong enough to win," is precisely the *kind* of thing we are looking for. It has just the right form—essentially the premises of a kind of rational argument often referred to as "practical reasoning."

But several reasons can be equally satisfactory in form, and one of them may be correct while the others may simply be wrong. William Marshal wanted material prizes in the form of booty and captives. Also, he wanted to position himself to win a noble heiress and so to acquire land and a title. Let us say that establishing a noble lineage and not victory for the English side or immediate material gain happened in this case to be the "real" reason why he entered the tournament. What is the difference between these various reasons when each has the same form—each explains the action rationally—but only one is *correct?* The heart of the difference cannot be that only heiress, land, and title were in Marshal's mind at the time. Only victory for the English side might have been in his mind, and we might still be convinced by a strong historical analysis that land and title were the real reasons. What can we possibly mean by "the real reasons" or by "correct" except to say that it was wanting land and title and not immediate material prizes or an English victory that were somehow the *cause* of his entering the tournament? We cannot easily account for this distinction and terminology except by the common notion of causality.

This very discussion, however, also gives us evidence that reasons and choices are *not* causes. For this analysis, which will be a turning point in the general argument, let us first consider the focal categories of psychological events only insofar as they are conscious, referring to them as "thoughts."

We begin with thoughts in the form of reasons. If we have several reasons for undertaking the same action and it happens that only one is causal, then the others are not causal. Extending this idea a bit, we have relentless empirical evidence from everyday life that reasons may not be efficacious. Most of the time, we have good, aware reasons for many *different* behaviors, but we will usually act on only one. What is different about the other reasons that they end up not being causes? I want to help my political party by going to a candidate reception, and I also want to repair some leaky shingles on the garage roof. I do the latter, but if reasons are causes, why did the first reason, which was a perfectly good reason indistinguishable in form from the second, not cause me to go to the reception?

Desires, which are an element of reasons, have no better claim.

First, neither the desire for a state of affairs nor the desire for an object would seem able in itself to cause a behavior because it designates no behavior. I may want to be an elected official, for example, or perhaps I want to have a better congressperson, but what does that in itself make me *do?* Many behaviors might be chosen to help me toward such goals, but the want itself designates none. Another kind of desire, the desire to perform a specific action, would seem to be more directive, but a second problem, the same as that just specified with respect to reasons, then becomes evident. Suppose that I have a desire to call a friend and find out how he or she is getting along. I may do it and I may not. We in fact desire all kinds of things, but we do not necessarily do anything about many of these desires, either at this moment or at any moment. Those desires, then, do *not* cause the behaviors that might satisfy them.

Last, consider the following group of similar thoughts: the willing, choice, decision, or intention to do something. For example, consider the intention or decision made by Mr. Jones on Friday to attend a candidate reception on Sunday. First, note that making the decision is itself an intentional behavior, so that if it is the cause as well, one must always decide to decide to decide, and so on back (Davidson 1980: 72). An initial response to this difficulty might be that decisions admittedly do not cause *all* intentional behaviors—we often do things (such as deciding itself) without consciously deciding to do them—but when we do decide, then we act, and we act intentionally *because* we have decided. But is that really true?

Even though Mr. Jones has decided, he does not, of course, go to the candidate reception immediately (on Friday). We may go further and say that on Friday the decision has not necessarily caused the behavior at all. We know that to be true because the behavior might never be carried out. For one, Mr. Jones might change his mind. But in addition, he might simply forget. If deciding on Friday caused going on Sunday, then changing one's mind or forgetting in the interim should not make a difference. If it does, it is hard to say what can be meant by the idea of causation since an instance of causation as we generally consider it cannot be erased. But even beyond that, he might not change his mind and might not forget at all and still thoroughly and awarely intend, now that Sunday is here, to carry out his decision, and yet the time to leave may come and go while he stands there thinking about it, never deciding *not* to go, but still not opening the closet door to get his coat—and it is highly likely that he will never know why (cf. Davidson

1980: 21–42). Most of us have had ample experience demonstrating that there are apparently factors we are unaware of capable of overriding, negating, or neutralizing decisions in this fashion. And in fact, one might decide to do something, not several days or even moments hence but right now, and still not do it, as for example, "I'm going to get my coat and leave for the reception right now" or "OK, this has gone far enough; I'm going to get out of bed right NOW!"

One might suppose, however, that if Mr. Jones does actually attend on Sunday, the decision on Friday was the cause or that if one does indeed get out of bed, it was that unequivocal, decisive thought that made one do it. If we would like to believe this, then we must ask, as we did with reasons and desires, why—if decisions, choices, willing, or intentions can be causes—are there so many times when precisely the same sort of intention, willing, choice, or decision was made but was not a cause, as is evidenced clearly by the fact that the corresponding behavior was never carried out?

There is, in short, a problem of irregularity in the argument that thoughts of all of these kinds are causes. The connection between our thought categories and the appropriate behaviors does not seem to be necessary or lawlike. It is, on the contrary, highly irregular and unreliable. For those who would hypothesize that human behavior is caused by these kinds of thoughts, the irregularity problem must be felt particularly keenly in the case of reasons because that category is a kind of last hope: desires in themselves—without linking with beliefs to form reasons—are disqualified because a thought that does not specify a behavior cannot be said to cause it, and deciding, choosing, willing, and intending are disqualified because they themselves are behaviors and so must be both cause and effect.

To show reasons as causes, one must somehow get around the irregularity problem, but there is another as well that we must also keep in mind. In referring to this problem area, Dennett (1971) speaks of a "debt of intelligence." The very property of a reason that saves it from disqualification along with decisions and choices—the fact that it is not itself an intentional behavior—is also a serious weakness. We can at least imagine that deciding, willing, or choosing to do something might itself push the behavioral button, but reasons are much less forceful. They do not command a behavior but only impart to it a "desirability characteristic" (Anscombe 1957, cited by Davidson [1980]: 8–9). We saw that a reason consists in the premises of a kind of rational argument referred to as practical reasoning, for example, "I wish to achieve Y and believe that doing X will achieve Y." The proper conclusion following from these premises would seem to be "Therefore, I will do X," but it has never been shown precisely how or why the premises of a rational argument must lead to this particular conclusion, let alone the action evoked by the conclusion (Dennett 1971). (The case here is no different from that of drawing the conclusion of an ordinary syllogism. Let us suppose that a person recognizes that all men are mortal and that Socrates is a man. If the person is too ignorant, narrow minded, unacculturated, inexperienced, or distracted to conclude "Therefore, Socrates is mortal," what are we to do [cf. Davidson 1980: 77]?) To get from the premises of a rational argument to the conclusion and from the conclusion that one should do X to the actual doing of X, it would seem that there would have to be a little person inside—an *intelligent* little person—capable of understanding how to reach such conclusions and move from those to the corresponding actions (Dennett 1971: 96). To conclude properly that reasons are causes without depending upon this black box, one must show the formal or physical apparatus that is capable of making these troublesome transitions without such leaps of intelligence. I suggest that this can in fact be done. We will leave this problem for the moment but show later that it is solved simultaneously with the irregularity problem.

Causes, Laws, and Human Behavior

Something causes the intentional behavior of the individual, so that if it is not reasons, decisions, or similar elements it becomes difficult to imagine what kind of event it could be. It is not a solution to resort to something like "neurons," although that is no doubt at least partially correct, because the neuronal behavior in question is not some random, capricious, self-generating set of events. Something makes the relevant neurons work the way they do, and it is hard to see that the physiological causes can result from anything other than the prior experience of the individual and his or her present purposes. Thus, a major obstacle to our inquiry is this irregularity that is so pervasive and clear. Because conscious reasons and decisions commonly occur without being followed by the appropriate behavior, doubt arises as to whether reasons can ever be physical causes. Are we not tied to the requirement that the relation be lawlike if it is physically causal?

As a first response, recall that physical causality is knowable in the singular instance without the benefit of laws. We must project to the particle level of neurons and muscle cells, but we can at least hypothesize that the relation between a conscious reason and its appropriate behavior in the individual instance is somehow translated into the relation between a force and a motion in this unfelt realm (cf. token identity and supervenience as in Kim 1979). That response is not adequate, however, because as we also noted we do have the Newtonian model. Although we do not depend on laws to know about physical causes, we do accept that such causes are part of the lawlike structure of the physical universe. Given such a structure, the question remains: can reasons be causes some of the time if they are not causes all of the time?

It is clear that for most ordinary physical entities the answer to this question is yes. Balls break windows some of the time, for example, but they surely do not do so all of the time. They do not even do so every time they are thrown at the window. There is a paradox here that is well accepted, although the reasoning behind it may not be well understood: a ball that is perfectly capable of breaking a certain window needn't *always* break the window, but when it does the event is *lawlike*.

One way in which the paradox may easily be understood is in terms of the idea of probabilistic encounters. *Physical causal laws do not cover the probabilistic encounter of one entity with another.* Whether force *X* will cause motion *Y* may depend on many encounters, up to the final one in which the force impinges upon the object in question. *It is only at that final stage that any law comes into play.* Given appropriate encounters (boy feels like throwing ball more than doing other things, ball does not meet shutter, ball hits window), a ball that is capable of breaking a window will break a window but not otherwise. Similarly, we may hypothesize that, given the proper encounters, a reason will cause the corresponding behavior but not otherwise. That is, many probabilistic things may have to happen first, but if they do then the reason will push appropriately upon the muscle control mechanism and the behavior will ensue. Just as in the case of balls, however, reasons may easily exist without having that effect. Thus, to address the original question, reasons may indeed be causes some of the time but not all of the time. It would seem that the erratic relation between reasons and behavior may simply reflect the role of encounters and need not be taken as indicating that reasons and similar thoughts cannot be causes at all.

Such a conclusion would be too hasty, however. The uncertainty interjected by encounters does not mean that no statement can be made relating objects such as balls and windows to the appropriate covering laws. This relationship is regularly shown, in fact, by ceteris paribus statements. We neutralize the complication introduced by encounters of all sorts, in one grand gesture, by stipulating that everything else be equal. All else being equal, if a ball breaks a window once, it will do so all the time. The same must apply in the case of thoughts and behavior.

Thus, the analysis brings us to a first stage conclusion: all else being equal, if certain kinds of thoughts physically cause behavior sometimes, they must do so all the time. If in some instances they do not, then to preserve the basic causal hypothesis one must look to the existence of conditions that differentiate the two kinds of cases—when reasons or other thoughts do cause behavior and when they do not—so that all else is seen *not* to be truly equal between them. The question, then, is whether such conditions can successfully be specified. The probable answer, we must recognize, is no, at least not in any meaningful sense, because to specify the conditions is to produce a law that makes intentional behavior predictable (Davidson 1980: 63–82), and the possibility of such an outcome is dubious.

In the various disciplines of social science, especially when the research is quantitative, investigators frequently do present a behavioral outcome to be explained, such as the adoption of innovations, plus a motive or reasons for undertaking the behavior, such as the status motive (Becker 1970) and some condition or set of conditions under which the relationship holds or is strong—in large organizations rather than small ones, for example. The hypothesized conditions might be environmental, social, cultural, political, or economic, or they might specify the prior experience or current beliefs, attitudes, or states of mind of the actor, or the behavior of others, and so forth. One sees from specifications of this sort that the investigator considers the core relationship not to hold universally without such a statement of qualifying conditions. The question is whether there is some faith or hope that it is universal *given* the qualifying conditions or given these plus one or two more that might yet be discovered. Cronbach (1975), for one, has claimed that such a hope is vain. I will argue in a later chapter that he is correct, but we can see initially that he is likely to be correct because it seems somehow essentially true that, no matter how long the list of conditions, it will always be possible to find at least one further condition—some sort of attitude or prior experience or cultural milieu or short-term social setting—that would lead to an exception.

Some philosophers, such as Malcolm (1982) and those reviewed by Davidson for a similar purpose in his essay "Freedom to Act" (1980: 76–79), have tried a different tack—one that avoids the apparently hopeless task of specifying detailed states of the agent's psyche, the environment, the behavior of others, and so on. Instead of focusing on the conditions under which a *particular kind* of reason will be causal, such as a reason to innovate or to go to war, this approach considers the conditions under which reasons in general—reasons on any subject— will cause the pertinent behavior. In this view, the conditions under which a reason or other thought will cause a person to do Y intention- ally are: that there be no countervailing factors, that the individual know how to do Y, be able to do Y, conclude that he or she should do Y, and not be prevented, and that he or she see no better way than Y to accomplish the pertinent goal. When all conditions of this sort prevail, then if the individual has a reason, has made a decision, and so on, to do Y, he or she will do Y. The objection to this, however, is simply that it is not true (cf. Davidson 1980: 77–78). For example, the person might *not* do Y intentionally in spite of all of these conditions because he or she suddenly carries out some other behavior at that time by accident or by habit instead. But beyond that sort of interference, and even more centrally for our purposes, a person might not do Y but might do Z intentionally instead of Y because he or she *also* has a reason for that. For example, a senator might want to vote "Yes" in order to satisfy her party as well as know how to vote "Yes," be able to vote "Yes," and so forth, but vote "No" instead in order to satisfy her constituency. Or, she might want to go to the chamber to vote in order to improve her atten- dance record but might nevertheless remain in her office at that moment in order to work on a speech. Or, an individual might indeed do Y (go to the chamber to vote) and do it intentionally but for a differ- ent reason that she *also* had, so that the subject reason (improve her attendance record) does not become a cause even though it is present and active. In sum, even when all of the noted conditions are satisfied, a reason may still not become a cause simply because it is overwhelmed by another reason.

On the other hand, this reasoning against the possibility of speci- fying the conditions under which behavior is lawlike does suggest the one condition that will apparently complete the set. If we were asked a question such as "If Senator X wanted to improve her attendance record, why did she stay to work on the speech instead?" most of us would almost certainly reply, "No doubt it was because she wanted the latter more!" We would seem, then, to have a full set of conditions if we added to those in the previous paragraph the simple qualifier ". . . and the subject want is *stronger* than all other currently active generators of behavior" (cf. Davidson 1980: 22–23). In fact, it seems that we *cannot* in principle have a full set of conditions, whether of the particular sort or the general, unless this strength factor be accounted for since presumably, under any conditions, other reasons that are equally reasons in every way can always compete with and potentially win out over the one we cite. This finding in regard to the strength factor is critical. It means that we have solved most of our problem. Yet, the solution toward which it points is perhaps unexpected, as the following paragraphs will show.

One detail of the proposal that has as yet gone unspecified is the measurement of the strengths whose existence we have just tentatively postulated. How does one know which want is strongest? Unfortunately, considering thoughts as potential causes, it seems clear that the want-strength is not part of the thought. There exists nothing at the aware level, in language or any other form, that might yield a measurement of this critical factor. It is true that we appear to ourselves at least sometimes to have a crude conscious sense of want-strength, so that there are some things that we want "very much" and others that we also want but "not desperately." There is no basis for thinking, however, that such measures are reliable. The behavioral outcome of a competition between want-strengths, even between two want-strengths that are apparently so unequal as "very much" and "not desperately," is really just a guess. What is apparently a most intense desire may frequently be overcome by one that is latent or one that does not appear to be very intense at all and turns out to be stronger than it seemed. And in general, when it comes to comparisons between innumerable wants such as improving the attendance record versus working on the speech or eating more versus being thinner, we find ourselves with little clue at all about which want is stronger and are even less knowledgeable about an absolute measure of each. Our basis for estimation of strength is likely to be an effort to guess what we will end by *doing* rather than a look inside for the intensity of a feeling or some similar quantity. Usually, we in fact need to wait to *see* what we do in order to learn what the ordering of want-strengths really was. If you got fat, then you must have wanted to eat more than you wanted to look svelte.

We could say that this does not matter, that strength need not be part of the thought but fulfills its role whether aware or not by being a condition under which the thought becomes causal. It does matter, however, when we remind ourselves that we are thinking here in terms of physical causation. The force that is the essence of the physical causation that thrusts this want into the ascendant position is seen to reside elsewhere than in the thought. At one critical point in the causal chain leading to intentional behavior the thought that might be supposed to represent the want, if it is part of this chain at all, is seen to be impotent. Neither that thought itself nor any other is capable of making this want the dominant one and thereby determinative. Something, however, does push the object of one want into ascendancy over the objects of all others at a given time, and this causal force is only roughly or partially revealed, if indeed it is revealed at all, by signs at the aware level.

Thus, thoughts do not play a role in fulfilling the strength condition. We are not always aware of all of the contending wants that might be about to determine our intentional behavior but only some of them. Among those of which we are aware because we have desires, reasons, and decisions in the form of thoughts, let us suppose for a moment that those thoughts themselves are causal. Which among the various aware reasons at a given time, however, will be determinative? Apparently, this is something we cannot control,[1] nor can we be sure that the next determinative reason will even be one of which we are presently aware. This status substantially diminishes our scientific interest in thoughts as causes. We still retain an interest in reasons and decisions, however, because they do not have to exist in the form of thoughts. It is therefore desirable to turn our attention to the nonconscious forms of these same psychological categories to see if they fare any better and to the physiological mechanism that produces intentional behavior so we can understand the nature of the strength factor.

---

1. This conclusion would appear to imply a fairly extreme position in the debate on the doctrine of free will. A chapter on this connection was in fact included in a prior draft of the present book but not retained because of insufficient probable appeal to the book's major audience. To those interested, however, the chapter is available from the author on request.

Nonconscious Reasons: The Affect-Object Paradigm

We often talk about "true" reasons, or "real" reasons, with the apparent implication that these are causal. A "true" reason is a reference to what is proposed to be the actual, rational explanation for a person's behavior, without particular regard for what the person behaving might think the explanation is, and indeed without the need for the agent to have had any thought about the behavior at all. Both as everyday observers and as social scientists, we commonly try to explain the behavior of individuals or groups in such a format. We might express our conviction, for example, that William Marshal entered the tournament because he wanted to affirm his loyalty to the English king. In providing this explanation, we might be aware that Marshal himself felt that he entered for that reason, we might be registering our opinion that his own, different explanation—that he wanted to win booty to share with his comrades in arms—was just a "rationalization," or we might have no idea at all what Marshal may have thought about the question, if anything. In social science, historical explanation is frequently of this variety, where a great deal of evidence besides actors' own statements or those attributed to them is amassed to arrive at an explanation for individual or group activity.

If one assumes that some physiological mechanism generates intentional behavior, then "true" reasons may be seen simply as a reference to what was going on in that physiological system at the time in question. In this perspective, not only an outside party but even the agent himself may function as an observer who imputes a reason. If one mistrusts one's own conscious processes in some connection (March 1978), then one might very well do a self-analysis, taking one's own statements and thoughts as evidence, but not conclusive evidence, and making inferences about the true reasons for one's own behavior: "In hindsight, I think that the real reason why I accepted the Dallas assignment was simply that I needed some time away from Washington." In this sense, the idea of *reasons* as causes has little to do with the subject of *thoughts* as causes. We recognize that people can have good, current reasons for doing things but without necessarily being aware of them. A critical question arises here, however, and that is whether the physiological system that produces intentional behavior has anything remotely to do with the notion of reasons or of decisions. If it does, and if we can also see that what we have called the "strength factor" is integrated somehow into these notions at the physiological level, then perhaps we can say that true reasons or decisions are causes.

The Affect-Object Paradigm

A description of the physiological system we seek does not appear in the literature of the fields one would think most likely. Clearly, too little is known from rigorous research to allow all of the pieces of such a large and intricate puzzle to be put together. There does exist in the literature of various fields, however, enough strong evidence to permit at least a rough sketch of this system to be put together, and it answers our major questions. Particularly noteworthy for us is the prominent role of affect in the system and its connection with the strength factor just discussed. The affect-object paradigm that I will outline here contains some significant gaps, but the evidence available suggests that it is correct in its essence.

The system that I will describe is, I propose, a set of natural causal events—what Malcolm (1982) and others call "mechanism" in this connection. We will see that it is not only more than but also somewhat different from a reason. Nevertheless, elements of the affect-object system are close enough to our idea of the form of a reason to illuminate how a physiological system can appear to function like a rational one and close enough as well to our ideas of the forms of desires, goals, and decisions to indicate how these may also at times appear to be the causes of behavior.

To begin, one must assume a physical space in the brain—not necessarily contiguous space—that I will refer to as the affect-object field. It is populated with neural representations of the objects that are contenders for influence over behavior at the moment. "Objects" may include material objects, concepts, thoughts, behaviors, words, and feelings. The population of objects generally shifts continuously, that is, some new objects may always enter and others leave. It is not certain what sorts of mechanisms determine which objects are in the field at a given time nor exactly how they are represented (a beginning on the latter issue has been made in Roitblat [1982]), but we may take as a starting point that the field includes current perceptions—objects seen, heard, felt, and so forth at the moment—as well as objects thought about at the moment though not actually present and at least some and perhaps all objects in short-term memory. While all objects currently represented in consciousness are also present in the affect-object field, the reverse is not true. The individual is aware of some of the items in the field, but may be unaware of much of its population at any given time. Last, some of the most important members of the population are objects perceived or recalled at the moment, but as they would appear in another form. For example, a skeptical and resistant colleague may be confronted in the present, but the same colleague convinced and supporting may also be a part of the field.

In conjunction with each object, there is imported as well a network of other objects that have become associated with the first by virtue of co-occurrence in past experiences, as in the theories proposed by Bower (1981: 134–36), Lang (1984), and Mishkin and his colleagues (Mishkin and Petri 1984; Mishkin, Malamut, and Bachevalier 1984). There is some tendency, I believe, to oversimplify these networks in current research. Webs of association may potentially be huge given that items of common experience must over time become associated with a very large number of other items of experience. At present, little is actually known about the physiological design of such associational matrices; it merely seems clear that they exist. I will plunge ahead nevertheless with a description of the main operative line of the system, assuming that the filling in of these details does not affect it materially. This is but one among many important areas, however, in which future research can clarify the results or output of the system by illuminating subroutines that are now obscure.

Prominent among the elements linked with each object is some associated affect—either an emotion currently felt and stimulated by the object, or a residue (not necessarily conscious) of past emotion, which I will call an "affect tag." The current association between the affect and the object has come about in one of two ways: (*a*) it is the result of a genetic program—certain smells or pheromones, for example, may genetically and therefore automatically have positive affect for all members of a species or (*b*) it is learned; that is, the object and the affect as a felt emotion either are now or have been components of a common experience. Affect attached by experience is always subject to change or updating by further experience, although there is evidence of a certain amount of built-in resistance to such change (see Zajonc 1980: 157). The evidence that affect is stored in memory in association with objects experienced is very strong (Zajonc 1980; Bower 1981; Gilligan and Bower 1984; Mishkin and Appenzeller 1987).

The objects in the affect-object field continually vie with one another by means of their attached affects and the affect tags on associated objects for influence over both attention (Lewis et al. 1981: 1168; Mishkin and Appenzeller 1987: 7) and the motor system (Bower 1981: 135; Zajonc and Markus 1984: 88–90). Affect is quantitative, varying in intensity (Lang 1984), and the strongest wins in this struggle for influence. This is true both of emotion that is currently being experienced and also of affect tags from memory, which are rarely experienced currently as emotions. When an object dominates the field by virtue of the strength of the affect attached either to itself or to an associated object, it becomes the orientation of signals sent to the motor system. This occurs in one of two ways, each of which embraces a set of diagonals in a two-by-two classification matrix (see table 1). The first is a *homeostatic* mechanism that acts to keep one doing what one is doing. It is activated when the dominant affect is either positive and associated with an object in current or imminent form (quadrant I; for simplicity, I suppress "or imminent" in the remainder of the discussion) or negative and associated with an object in some noncurrent form (quadrant IV). The second way, on the other hand, is a way of producing *change*. It is evoked when the dominant affect is either negative and associated with an object in current form (quadrant III) or positive and not current (quadrant II).

First, if the dominant affect is positive and is paired with an object in current form, such as feeling warm and cozy in bed, the signals emanating from the brain and organizing the motor system for behavior (see Gallistel 1980: 210–334) keep the body functioning in the current pattern until satiety is achieved or there is distraction by stronger affect elsewhere. For example, if you are warm and comfortable under the covers, you stay there for a while; if you are hungry and have begun to eat, you continue for a while; or if your interest has been aroused in a

TABLE 1. The Four Types of Affect-Object Dyads

Affect	Object	
	Current	Not Current
Positive	I (Warm in bed)	II (Box open)
Negative	III (Hand being squeezed)	IV (Muddy shoes)

book or a problem, you keep at it for a while. In other words, the inclination to persist in certain behavior in conjunction with current emotion or affect tags is built in, universal, and automatic. Similarly, if the affect is negative and paired with the memory of an object in some form that is not current, the body is kept away from experiencing the object in that form. One is maintained in a physical attitude of avoidance. For example, the object may be your own shoes covered with mud. If a large muddy patch appears in your way and stimulates the entry of this object into the field, you circle the perimeter of the patch as you go rather than walking right through it.

What if the strongest affect in the field is positive but paired with an object in noncurrent form—for example, the warm hearth when you are out in the cold? Or what if the strongest affect is a negative one attached to an object as it is currently being experienced, such as a conversation with a tiresome colleague? In these cases, instead of maintaining the individual in the present behavior pattern relative to the object, the signals are such as to tend to bring about a change. This is a critical function for study because it is so strongly suggestive of what is commonly meant by the pursuit of a goal—attaining some different status that either will provide satisfaction or permit an escape from the experience of distress. There is not enough direct evidence to propose with confidence a mechanism that leads from the physiological status represented by these two quadrants to the actual pursuit of change. There is, however, enough evidence to warrant a suggestion, one that is both simple and plausible. I suggest that the mechanism that performs this function is what Simon and his colleagues call a "means-end analysis" (Simon 1977; Simon, Newell, and Shaw 1979). Our perspective and purpose are slightly different from Simon's, so that we might rename it, accordingly, a "means-end procedure."

In trying to produce a computer program that would solve a certain class of problems, Simon studied how a population of subjects went about solving theorems in symbolic logic. Essentially, he asked them to solve the problems and to say out loud what they were doing as they went along. He found that they tended to juxtapose some simple beginning statement *known* to be valid with the end point—the symbolic statement to be *proven* valid—and then to perform legitimate operations on the first to try to transform it into the second. If it could successfully be transformed, then the end statement was a valid theorem. The students compared the two statements and, if different (which of course they were to begin), made a legitimate transformation of the first, compared again, made another transformation if the result were a closer match, undid the transformation and tried another one if the result were not a closer match, and so on. Transformations and important dimensions of comparison were selected by various heuristic devices, there being no known formulas or algorithms except endless trial and error on which to rely. Thus, a successful result was not guaranteed but had a decent probability both of being produced and of being produced very efficiently relative to the systematic, exhaustive trial-and-error method.

Simon frequently repeats that the logic of the means-end procedure is declarative, by which I take him to mean that no intellective intentionality or semantic capability is necessary to pursue it. The mechanism, in other words, might be duplicated on an ordinary computer, and in fact it was, very successfully. However, it is also true that overall purposefulness—notification that the input was a certain sort of problem to be solved—was exogenous. Somehow, there had to be an instruction to put this input into the role of the endpoint of a routine— to adopt a *goal* in connection with it. "Here is a statement to be proved valid or invalid—Go to it!" Neither we nor computers, after all, put all the statements we receive into the role of the endpoint of a means-end procedure. This instruction did not arise from within the design of the problem-solving system itself. It definitely had to be given to the computer by the investigator. Human beings, on the other hand, are fully capable of arriving at such an instruction (*intention*) themselves and of doing so only for *particular* statements or other objects and not all of them. How do we determine which states of the world that occur to us will be goals—the objects of effort? The faculty is a marvel; it will probably always separate organic systems from computers in terms of the capability of a broad range of choice in the allocation of effort. I will return to this problem of the roots of intentionality momentarily.

I suggest that the means-end procedure is a general program built into the neurological system not only as a problem-solving mechanism in humans but as a behavior-producing mechanism in all mammals and perhaps other animals whose behavior depends in part on affect and associative memory (cf. Mackie 1980: 281–82; also see Scheier and Carver 1982: 159–61, for the scheme of a similar mechanism of behavioral guidance that is based, as is the case with the means-end procedure, on cybernetic control). Call the starting point A-position and the end point B-position. When the strongest affect in the field is a positive tag on the noncurrent form of an object (e.g., the warm hearth far away or, to take a simpler example, a box open rather than closed), the object in that form is thrust into the B-position of the means-end mechanism. The object in its current form, which sometimes means its absence altogether, is placed in A-position and the procedure automatically commences and runs according to the programmed routine of comparison, transformation, comparison, acceptance or rejection, and so forth. The means of transformation from one state to the other (getting oneself closer to home and hearth or getting the box from closed to open), which are the very caused behaviors that concern us in this discussion, are drawn from experience, having occurred in some form together with this object or a similar one in the past, having also a neural representation in memory, and being now an element in the web of associations around that object (Lang 1984; Lane et al. 1995). Perhaps several behaviors have accomplished all or part of the task before. A person may have obtained a certain sort of information from a source in the past by telephone, by mail, by computer message, and in person. Which one is now selected by the means-end procedure? There may well be a certain amount of pure randomness here. Frequently, however, aspects of the behavioral means for effecting the transformation from A to B become objects in the affect-object field themselves. A few frustrating or unpleasant recent attempts to do business with a large organization by telephone may now render the telephone option something to be avoided, like the muddy patch. A recent feeling of satisfaction with computer messaging as a novelty may, for a time, give it a strong positive character, like the warm hearth or open box, even though it is here a means rather than an end from the perspective of the need to obtain information. Moreover, the behavior selected may itself be nonspecific, as it is in this example, so that a subbehavior must also be selected by the system in the same way. For example, if regular mail is selected, there is a stamp to be obtained, and the letter must be delivered to a mailbox. There is a hierarchy, in other words, in which behaviors selected by the means-end procedure themselves may become momentary objects in the field for the selection of subbehaviors, and so on until the end point is reached, effecting a final transfer back to the main routine of the affect-object field. In the meanwhile, there may be an interruption. The original affect-object dyad may exit from the field for some reason (so that we sometimes "forget what we were trying to do"), or there is distraction by virtue of the ascendancy in strength of a new affect-object dyad. Last, even if the original object keeps returning to B-position for a good while as behaviors are recalled and perhaps tried, still, a successful result clearly is not guaranteed. Without experience relevant for the present context, for example, one is likely to fail or at least to be very slow. This sort of failure produces frustration, a major form of distress, so that the negative emotion on the behavior per se begins to vie for dominance with the positive affect on the original goal, and the normal workings of the affect-object system will in this way eventually cause the individual who does not succeed to give up the effort.

The idea of the function of "B-position" in the means-end procedure is supported by Griffin's notion of an "inherited template" (Griffin 1984: 114–17). In reviewing research on certain apparently intelligent behaviors of animals, including insects, Griffin concludes that animals may inherit species-dependent templates. These are neural representations of such things as nests, songs, traps (to snare prey), and other critical artifacts. When triggered, the templates serve as models to guide goal-seeking behavior (such as nest building, etc.) in cybernetic fashion. The B-position hypothesis just proposed simply extends this notion to cover templates that are not inherited but come from experience by way of memory.

The means-end procedure is similarly evoked when the strongest affect is negative and is paired with an object as currently experienced, so that the associated object in some form that will *not* produce negative affect is put into B-position, the current status into A-position, and so on. For example, when a person's hand is being squeezed hard by someone or something, the hand's *not* being squeezed goes into B-position. Perhaps a more vivid variant concerns negative affect on an object in a form that is not actually current but imminent. The example comes to mind of Mr. Allnut (Humphrey Bogart) in the movie *The African Queen* (20th Century Fox 1951), who, because of negative affect on imminent death by thirst and starvation both for himself and his Rosie (Katherine Hepburn), gets back into the swampy river to continue towing the boat forward, even though he has just emerged from it covered with slimy leeches. The negative affect on the leeches is strong but that on the consequences of remaining marooned is stronger.

Above all, note the critical role of affect in this process. It is the physical representation of the strongest affect currently experienced or recalled that places an associated object in B-position of a means-end procedure. This is the component of the system that supplies what we earlier called the strength factor. Thus, a "goal" or "motive" here is not an intellective or spiritual entity but the material, neural representation of an object-status placed in the B-position of a programmed means-end procedure by virtue of being associated with the strongest affect in the affect-object field. With this component added (which of course depends entirely on the organic capability of experiencing affect and associating it with objects), the logic of the system does become fully declarative. And it is this faculty of using affect to determine what one's goals and priorities will be that computers do not share.

I hope by the above description to contribute an element that has been lacking as background in the long-standing controversy about reasons as the causes of action, namely, one concrete example of a conceivable physiological mechanism that produces ordinary intentional behavior with nothing more than plain material parts. The traditional discussion has been hampered, I think, by the lack of attention to and shared information about what the components of such a system might need to be—how it might actually work. A related aspect of this book as a whole is the derivation of a basis of doubt whether the core of such a physiological system may be controlled by thought in any form. By the "core of the system" I mean the activation of behavior by purpose—the "Go to it!" element—that element that is represented in the affect-object paradigm by the thrust of an object into B-position by virtue of the strength of its associated affect. Last, the existence of a functional position such as B-position, as well as the comparison of strengths or valences necessary to place something there and the hierarchical or nested means-end procedures that must build a complex means to the end—all, I believe, are in harmony with the particulars that are already known about the neurological architecture of the production of learned behavior (see Gallistel 1980: 210–334).

The affect-object paradigm is a social science hypothesis that specifies a type of process. I would classify it under the rubric of "encounter theory" (cf. "process theory" in Mohr 1982: 35–70, 213–17). To see why, consider that the output of the process of concern is the answer to the question "What among the many possibilities at this moment will the organism actually do?" Physiological causality is clearly important in this connection, but the essence of the hypothesis from the standpoint of this question is not any of the causal events involved but a probabilistic encounter—a meeting, a happening. This is an encounter between several objects associated with affects of varying strengths, so that one object emerges as dominant. That is how the choice among possible actions is made. If some of the objects and strengths happened to be different, so might the behavior. To suggest an analogy, reproduction is a similar process, where physiological causality is again prominent but where the core of the output-producing mechanism (the output here being a new organism with one particular set of traits rather than many other possible sets) is a probabilistic encounter between a sperm cell and an egg cell, each with its own individual complement of genes.

The present hypothesis is derived from the results of research in several different traditions, there being for a variety of reasons a relative dearth of research that targets the relation of affect to behavior directly. Nevertheless, proposals quite similar in tone to the affect-object paradigm have been made by Staats (1975: 78–113), Sinnamon (1982), and Hursh (1980, cited in Sinnamon 1982). Besides the work of Simon and his colleagues on the means-end procedure (Simon 1977; Simon et al. 1979) and the broad range of studies on the functioning of the neurological system in complex behavior that was organized and summarized in 1980 by Gallistel, four categories of findings have been important in shaping the hypothesis.

The first is the "anhedonia" hypothesis concerning the effect of neuroleptic (antipsychotic) drugs on operant behavior. The general observation, confirmed in a large number of studies, is that rats that have been conditioned by rewards to push levers, traverse mazes, and so forth, do not perform the conditioned behaviors as readily, and eventually not at all, after fairly mild doses of these drugs. The studies on rats are supported by studies of various sorts on other animals as well as on humans (Wise 1982: 50–51). Wise organizes the experimental evidence from his own and other laboratories to refute the hypothesis that the drugs simply interfere with motor competence and to advance instead the anhedonia hypothesis. This theory would explain non- or underperformance of the conditioned responses as owing to the fact that the reward in each case is not experienced as pleasurable under the influence of the neuroleptic drugs. The basic reasoning underlying the hypothesis is that the drugs are known to block dopamine receptors in the limbic system (midbrain) and a range of other structures within the brain, many of which are known to be implicated in the production and regulation of affect (Mueller 1984). Dopaminergic pathways mediate between sensory and affective structures and between affective and motor structures (Mueller 1984; German 1982; Panksepp 1982). Thus, under the blocking effect of the drugs, the emotion of enjoyment generally resulting from such rewards as food, stimulants, and so forth is not felt. In this way, the association of lever pressing and so forth with pleasure is soon erased, and the affective centers do not stimulate the usual motor responses.

The evidence in favor of the core of the anhedonia hypothesis is persuasive (see the broad range of commentaries following Wise's 1982 article). One must conclude that for a broad class of important behavior—behavior that in intentional terminology would be called reward-seeking or discomfort-avoiding—performance at least in some instances is stimulated by and is critically dependent on affective inputs from the limbic system or other dopaminergic structures.

The plausibility of the conclusion is strengthened by the research of Mishkin and his colleagues on brain-lesioned animals (Aggleton and Mishkin 1986; Mishkin and Appenzeller 1987), which begins to show the precise roles of limbic system and diencephalic structures, especially the amygdala and the hypothalamus, in the affect-centered regulation of behavior.

The latter scholarly sources in fact belong to a second category of information—research to establish the roles of particular brain structures in emotion and memory, primarily by manipulating those structures directly in animals. In the process, the role of affect in behavior is clearly implicated. That is, it becomes clear that the amygdala and the hypothalamus influence behavior, both "on-line" and through memory, and it is evident at the same time that the observations of behavior so influenced are also observations of affect. Aggleton and Mishkin (1986: 285, 291–92) cite many examples of research in which behavior is clearly influenced and affect is clearly implicated: amygdalectomized animals simply fail to react to stimuli that ordinarily would be meaningful, such as being captured or restrained, looming objects, air puffs, and pinching, and positive social advances by other animals (grooming, embracing). Mothers even showed a lack of maternal care. Through ingenious research protocols, memory is shown to be the slave of affect tags mediated by the amygdala (Spiegler and Mishkin 1981, cited in Mishkin et al. 1984: 67). Finally, these scholars cite a range of studies of human beings in which there was limbic system damage due to disease, accident, or surgery. The same effects were evident, that is, "a remarkably flattened affect similar if not identical to the hypo-emotionality observed in the experimental animal subjects." Behavior and the expression of affect become so intertwined as to begin to meld together, both conceptually and phenomenologically.

In sum, this second stream of research suggests that intact affective pathways make the difference between behaving in certain ways in response to stimuli and showing what we would essentially call no reaction—not for all behavior, indeed, but for those forms that we are most prone to categorize as "intentional," even in nonhuman species. Mishkin and his colleagues have been primarily interested in nailing down the concrete functions of one brain structure, the amygdala. To us, their research indicates that certain brain structures mediate in certain specific ways between sensory inputs, memory, and behavioral outputs. Thereby, the research also indicates the outlines of an affect-centered neurochemical architecture for the generation of intentional behavior.

A third source of evidence centers on research on human subjects involving the relation between affect and cognition. Dienstbier's work (1984), for example, may be seen as demonstrating the critical impor-tance of the *link* between affect and object, as opposed to either element alone, in determining certain behavior. He concludes from several care-ful studies that "one's ideas about the source and meaning of one's emotional experience determine . . . the impact of that experience on behavior" (508).

Other research in this category includes an extensive literature on the relation between mood, on the one hand, and memory and other cognitive elements on the other. The investigators active in the study of mood-related cognitive and motor activity explicitly consider mood to be an affective state. In the perspective we have been using here, mood would seem frequently to be currently experienced affect that is a residue from recent experience—a sort of afterglow or, in the wine taster's terminology, a "lingering finish." As such, its attachment to a particular object is secondary to its striking role in the internal struggle of affects. Bower (1981) suggests that affects vie for dominance. Zajonc and Markus (1984) present an innovative and very persuasive case for the proposition that an emotional state inhibits the ascendance of its opposite by having control of muscle tonus and other physiological manifestations. Thus, emotion has an inertia, frequently known as mood, so that the strongest affect in the current affect-object field may become so because some opposite affect is cancelled or overpowered by lingering mood. The studies of mood, cognition, and behavior bring the role of affect into high relief. For Bower (1981), for example, the primary implications of a series of such studies he reviewed are (*a*) that affect tags are stored with experiences and (*b*) that these tags are of critical importance for later use of the experiences. Mueller similarly concludes, but mainly on the basis of physiological research (1984: 99): "It appears that sensory experience achieves meaning or attains permanence in memory only to the extent that it is paired, however indirectly, with the experience of pleasure or pain at a core-brain or 'visceral' level."

Tomkins (1981), reviewing a career emphasizing the study of affect, and Zajonc (1980), reviewing a broad range of literature bearing on affect, came to several mutually supportive conclusions on the relation between affect and cognition. The evidence is found to be strong that the physiological systems involved in the processing of affect and cognitions are distinct. Processing time in the affective system is far more rapid. In general, recall accuracy is strongly influenced by affect. One may conclude that the affective system possesses characteristics that are necessary for the use of experience in the production of behavior and that in some critical ways the affect system is so used. MacLean (cited by Mueller [1984]: 116) concludes: "We try to be rational, intellectual, to be wary of our emotions. But as far as we have been able to tell to this day—and this is probably the most fundamental thing we have learned, or ever will learn about the nervous system, the only part of the brain that can tell us what we perceive to be real things is the limbic brain."

A final source of suggestive evidence bears on the role of affect in the setting of priorities. Simon (1967) concluded long ago on the basis of his own research and that of others that, as summarized by Scheier and Carver (1982: 177), "Emotion causes an interruption of ongoing processing, and *calls for a rearrangement of goal priorities.* More specifically, the presence of a strong emotion seems to represent a call for the goal to which that emotion is relevant to be accorded a higher priority than whatever goal is presently being pursued" (italics in original). Another perspective on this comes from quite a different kind of evidence. Mueller (1984: 110–13) cites the conclusion of several researchers in areas relevant to temporal lobe epilepsy that many of the symptoms of this disease result from a hyperconnectivity between sensory and motor structures. This seems in turn to be mediated by a hyperactivity across dopaminergic synapses involving structures that are critical in the processing of affect, especially the amygdala (which forms part of the temporal lobe). In temporal lobe epilepsy, sensory experiences that otherwise would result in little or no affect stimulate strong affect instead. The mechanism appears to be a "random pairing of motivationally neutral sensory stimuli with states of limbic arousal" (Mueller 1984: 112). These experiences occupy the attention of the patient and distort behavioral priorities. Many patients become extremely philosophical or religious because of the vastly increased and more diffuse "meaning" that life takes on under the pathology. Thus, we can see that by investing some experience in the normal, healthy individual with little or no affect, the limbic brain enables life to proceed by allowing the person or animal to ignore a great deal of nonessential sensory experience; otherwise, we would be overwhelmed by detail. And similarly, by imbuing the experience with more and less affect according to its nature and intensity, the limbic system determines priorities for influence in neurologic structures that mediate behavior. Simultaneously, it also determines priorities for attention. Based on chemical and neurological studies, Mishkin and his colleagues (Lewis et al. 1981: 1168; Aggleton and Mishkin 1986: 295–96) have hypothesized that neural projections from the amygdala back to sensory centers in the cortex (contrary to most research, which has involved fibers running in the opposite direction) serve as an affect-attention mechanism, engaging attention on the particular sensory perceptions that arouse affect.

In short, structures do exist that process a very large range of experience in terms of affect and affect strength. Moreover, the structures operate on the basis of links between representations of affect and objects. Finally, certain apparently broad categories of behavior depend unequivocally and critically on these structures for their performance, so that it may meaningfully be said that the structures "generate" the behavior in question. What I have done principally is to organize what is known into a hypothesized, integrated mechanism and to propose that the mechanism is capable of ordering and generating all of the behavior we commonly think of as intentional.

Behaviorism and the Paradigm

It seems clear that much behavior is purposeful. How could it be so if it were not organized by what we generally think of as purpose? The affect-object paradigm is the answer offered here. Physiologically, the affect associated with an object is responsible for attention's and motor responses' being directed toward that object. Behaviorism in psychology has offered another answer, one that would seem to be an alternative to the affect-object paradigm. Indeed, the affect-object paradigm might seem to many to be simply a variant of what has already been offered by the behaviorists. It is in fact close to the behaviorist solution in that it does not depend on reasons in the form of thoughts or similar mentalistic concepts—a feature that gets to the very identity of behaviorism—but it departs crucially from that solution in that it does find the explanation for intentional behavior inside the head of the individual rather than outside in the environment. In this light, the two could not be more purely opposed.

The essence of behaviorism, from Watson (1930) and Hull (1943) to Skinner (1953), is that behavior can be explained, indeed should be explained, as the result of conditioning reinforcement from the environment. In the presence of a stimulus, we respond in a certain way. The more the world rewards us with pleasure for that response, the more likely we are to repeat it in the presence of the same stimulus and similarly for the avoidance of pain. To predict behavior, then, we must use the environmental stimuli. Knowing the conditioning of a particular boy, for example, we may know that if he confronts a large dog he will make some avoidance maneuver.

What we should *not* use to predict behavior according to these scholars is thoughts and feelings—goals, reasons, wanting, and the like. At best, these are "intervening variables" between environment and behavior, and to use them alone as predictors is to use an incomplete causal chain (Skinner 1964). Moreover, the measurement of internal states is unreliable, perhaps inherently so, whereas the environment that has produced those thoughts and feelings, as well as the behaviors, is material, tangible, and objectively measurable (Skinner 1964). In the behaviorist view, we *can* develop a science of behavior by this objective path. By cleaving to mentalism, however, we will only fail to do so.

The problem of behaviorism in light of the affect-object paradigm is that it oversimplifies. If only one stimulus presented itself at a time—a medium rare steak, a book on the opera—we might possibly be able to predict accurately what an individual will do by understanding his or her history of conditioning. Stimuli regularly present themselves *many* at a time, however; some being presented only from memory. What then does the individual do? Consider Davidson's answer to a similar question with respect to reasons:

> Generalizations connecting reasons and actions are not—and cannot be sharpened into—the kind of law on the basis of which accurate predictions can reliably be made. If we reflect on the way in which reasons determine choice, decision, and behavior, it is easy to see why this is so. What emerges, in the *ex post facto* atmosphere of explanation and justification, as *the* reason frequently was, to the agent at the time of action, only one consideration among many, *a* reason. Any serious theory for predicting action on the basis of reasons must find a way of evaluating the relative force of various desires and beliefs in the matrix of decision; it cannot take as its starting point the refinement of what is to be expected from a single desire. (1980: 15–16, italics in original)

> What prevents us from giving necessary and sufficient conditions for acting on a reason also prevents us from giving serious laws connecting reasons and actions. To see this, suppose we had the sufficient conditions. Then we could say: whenever a man has such-and-such beliefs and desires, and such-and-such further conditions are satisfied, he will act in such-and-such a way. There are no serious laws of this kind. . . . What is needed in the case of action, if we are to predict on the basis of desires and beliefs, is a quantitative calculus that brings all relevant beliefs and desires into the picture. There is no hope of refining the simple pattern of explanation on the basis of reasons into such a calculus. (1980: 233)

The crucial point is that if we are to understand why a person (or other animal) does what he or she does intentionally at the moment, we must in principle look *inside*, at the various objects that happen to be contending and at the affect strengths associated with each. If we are prevented from doing that by limitations in measurement technology, then so much the worse. We can only guess at what the behavior will be. The causal mechanism is inside, where it depends critically on webs of association and the strength factor. The role of any given environmental stimulus in the determination, prediction, and understanding of behavior, regardless of past reinforcement and conditioning, depends on whether it is represented at the time inside the head, in the affect-object field, as well as on what is associated with it and what else is represented in the affect-object field at the same moment. Looking outside even in a minimally complex situation above the level of a Skinner box, one sees only a plethora of "things"; there is no way to tell which are represented in the affect-object field, in what dimensions, with what associated memories, and with what strengths of attached affects. For example: It is evening and Marjorie sees a chemistry textbook and a television set. There was also a problem in philosophy that she was unable to solve earlier in the day. Further, there is a stain on the wall and precisely two throw pillows on the couch. What does she do? It is surely difficult if not impossible for the behaviorist to answer, even knowing ten or twenty of Marjorie's reinforcement histories. In the perspective of the affect-object paradigm, what the behaviorist solution fails to take into account is that the behavior-generating mechanism depends crucially on the intervention of an *encounter*—the particular population of the affect-object field, including all relevant associations conjoined with philosophy problems, throw pillows, and so on—and not only on one or more particular histories of reinforcement.

Affinity of the affect-object paradigm toward two opposing theories is suggested. Because the encounter is inside the head and because elements of the affect-object system are strongly reminiscent of the ideas of goal, want, decision, and reason, the paradigm has salient points in common with the cognitive model. At the same time, as in behaviorism, it is purely mechanistic. It operates without purposeful thought at the trigger point and emphasizes the role of past experience, especially of pleasure and pain, in determining present behavior. Given this mix of characteristics, it is clear that the affect-object paradigm is neither the one nor the other but stands independently somewhere in between the cognitivist and behaviorist approaches to explanation.

Operative Reasons as Causes

The affect-object paradigm offers a mechanism that may clearly be seen as causal in its physiological description while at the same time harboring the elements of rationality. In the rational-psychological realm, a reason (Davidson 1980) or purposive explanation (Malcolm 1982) consists roughly in a want (e.g., William Marshal's desire to indicate his loyalty to the English king) and a belief (e.g., the belief that entering the tournament would accomplish that). A want is represented in the affect-object system in terms of affect associated with an object in non-current form, such as strong positive affect on the informed or enlightened king. This affect-object dyad is a direct and simple physical embodiment of one of the primary meanings of "want" or "desire" in ordinary language—I want the king to know that I am loyal. A belief is represented by the presence of the neural representation of a certain behavior (entering a tournament) in the network of memory objects associated with a central object (the king's perceptions of loyal subjects), so that the behavioral memory is available to be selected by the means-end procedure. That is, the memory of knights' having successfully signaled loyalty in the past by entering tournaments gets at least close to what we mean by the belief that entering a tournament is likely to signal loyalty. Thus, if we claim that William Marshal had a particular reason and do not care what if anything he actually was thinking about, we may consider ourselves to be referring by the term *reason* precisely to these events in the affect-object system—positive affect on showing loyalty to the English king and the availability in ready memory of entering a tournament as a potentially efficacious behavior.

It is worth pausing for a moment to remark upon the approach of the causal and the rational in the affect-object system, for other common causal mechanisms in nature and art are not configured in this way at all. The causal connection between the switch and the light, for example, has no hint of rationality in it, but the similar physical connection between the affect-object system and a behavior is based fundamentally on a selection of ends and means—ends on a salience criterion (we select the end that is most desired) and means at least to some extent on an efficacy criterion (we select a means that is supposed to work). In this way, the affect-object system would appear a good part of the time to operate as a rational, intentional mechanism. It is capable of creating the kind of thing we are prone to call "goal" and selecting behavior that has a good chance of achieving it. I say "a good part of the time" because the affect-object system will equally, from time to time, select behavior that we might well call irrational, such as telling off your boss or bringing your country to the brink of a war that you are almost bound to lose. Still, although perhaps not conforming to an archetypal economic or decision-theoretic idea of rational behavior, the system strikes us as essentially rational in a real-life, human sort of way.

In much the same fashion as reasons, other categories of event that we sometimes consider to be causes of behavior are also represented in the affect-object system. The idea of deciding, choosing, or intending to do something, for example—all closely similar in meaning (Meiland 1970: 55–65)—is represented (*a*) in the transmuting of what was merely a want (that the king be informed) into a goal of behavior by the thrust of a dominant object into B-position of the means-end procedure, thereby "choosing" or "deciding upon" a goal or (*b*) in the selection of a certain behavior (entering the tournament) as a means of transformation from A to B within that procedure, thereby "deciding" to do a certain something associated with attaining the desired state.

We may now pause as well to clarify what we mean by the term *intentional behavior.* When our muscles or organs behave in certain ways under certain conditions in response to habit, accidents, physical forcing, or hot frying pans, we do not count it as intentional behavior. What we in fact mean by intentional behavior is behavior that is produced by just such a mechanism as the affect-object system, except that we would generally describe it in psychological terms (want, goal, etc.) rather than physiological terms (affect on object, shunted to B-position, etc.). In these somewhat unsatisfactory terms, then, and in briefest version, *intentional behavior is behavior that one performs in order to achieve a particular state that one prefers.* (Cf. Katz 1982: 60: "So we might allow behavior to be called 'motivated' just when past or present hedonic [or, more broadly, affective] arousal figures essentially in its etiology.")

In the unaware sense of the term *reasons,* by which it refers to the affect-object system, reasons would definitely *appear* to be causes, with the caveat that in so saying we have claimed nothing at all about the control of behavior by thoughts. I suggest that we cannot even go quite that far, however. Strictly speaking, and in a sense that is noteworthy, unaware reasons are not truly physical causes. They are only factual causes because the natural events that are designated by the unaware reason are not quite enough to account physically for the behavior. This same reasoning would also disqualify aware reasons—reasons as thoughts—and is related to my prior discussion of the strength element, as we will now see.

Just as I have noted with respect to wants, a reason generally occurs in the context of other reasons; that is, there are several things that one might do at any given moment, some of them oriented toward different goals and some of them perhaps being alternative ways of achieving the same goal. The onset of the reason—the entry of its components into the affect-object system—is an event. At that point, the subject reason is no more causal than the other affect-object dyads and behaviors in the system. As we have seen, each imparts only a desirability characteristic to some possible behavior. For example, "accepting the Dallas assignment" becomes a desirable thing to do when it is associated with the affect-object dyad that translates as "the felt need to spend some time away from Washington." But that does not mean that it will be done. If it is done, and if we are to impute to the actor a set of events that is causal with respect to this behavior, we must in fact add to the onset of the true reason two additional, distinct events, namely, (a) that this affect component (the want connected with getting away) be selected out because it is the strongest, or in some other way overpowers the others, so that the object in question is transferred to B-position and (b) that this behavior (accepting the Dallas assignment) be seized upon by the means-end procedure as a means of transformation of the world from A into B. These additional events may be thought of in psychological terms as decisions: the decision to pursue a certain end, such as getting away from Washington—a goal decision—and the decision to implement in a certain way, such as by accepting the Dallas assignment—a means decision.

Thus, to impute a "reason" that is truly causal, whatever vocabulary might be used, is actually to impute to the actor a reason plus two decisions—three separate events. To get from the onset of the reason to the first decision, the one that makes a goal out of the want, depends on an encounter: that object is shunted to B-position which happens to be associated with the strongest affect at the time. To get from the goal decision to the means decision depends on a selection mechanism of some sort. This may again involve a comparison on the basis of affect, or possibly a random draw, or it might be some other selection mechanism that research has not yet discovered. In case only one means is available in the network, that means would simply be selected and imported into the means-end procedure, but that nevertheless involves a "decision." The selection event is different from the behavior's existing as a possibility—even the only possibility.

It is now easy to see why the search for the conditions under which reasons become causes fails categorically, or equivalently, why there are no laws connecting intentional behavior with psychological concepts such as reasons—even unaware reasons (cf. Davidson 1980: 215). We do not have the *general*-level law that whenever a person has a reason to do something he or she will do it because whether the person does it or not depends upon an encounter and usually in fact on several. As we have seen, there cannot be a strict or fully predictive causal law connecting any X and Y if the connection depends upon encounters. The zap of interference with the outcome could come from any corner of the universe, up to the final moment, so that the potential law would fail to be fulfilled. Chiefly, in our case, whether any given reason to do something will become causal depends in part on what *other* reasons happen to be present and on the strength of their associated affect tags, just as whether or not a full house will prevail depends on what *other* hands were dealt in the same round. Moreover, whether a given reason will produce behavior depends as well on other factors that are *not* reasons, such as external interference and internal generators of nonintentional behavior. Last, we note that the particular collection of other factors that is present, reasons and nonreasons, is probabilistic in the sense that it is never determined by the presence of the subject reason. Other potential causes (different reasons, habits, distractions, accidents, etc.) are borne into the picture at least in part by different causal streams.

Further, we do not have laws about content-specific reasons and behaviors, again because of the nest of imponderable encounters. For example, there is no law connecting the status motive with innovation because encounters—depending on the happenstance of prior experience and current context—govern whether the status motive as reason and innovation as action will become connected as cause and effect for any given person in any given instance. Clearly, there are many regularities that we label "laws" in social science, such as the law of supply and demand and the iron law of oligarchy. According to the present analysis, they cannot be strict laws (I doubt that anyone would claim them to be such) but are rather limited regularities of some sort. We will see in chapter 5 that they cannot be probabilistic laws either because even these, I will argue, are not possible in social science. Whether they might be *important* regularities, even if limited, is a different issue entirely, to be considered in chapters 4 through 6.

The closest we may come to a causal "law" that does hold connecting reasons with behavior is the following: with reservations, whenever a strongest reason and its two appropriate decisions occur, then so does the corresponding behavior. More fully, whenever you want Y more than anything else and believe that X will achieve Y, and decide therefore to pursue Y, and also decide on some basis to do so by means of X, then, barring interference with the mechanism, you will do X, and in so doing will perform an intentional behavior. With the caveat that the wants, beliefs, reasons, and decisions here refer purely to physiological events and not to thoughts, the "law" does indeed hold. It simply states in other terms that the affect-object system is the mechanism that produces intentional behavior. I place "law" in quotes to remind us that what is described here is a mechanism and that neither a natural nor an artificial mechanism can ever be technically lawlike. It is always subject both to malfunction and to interruption by an external force at the final or any prior instant.

In one detail, a strong empirical claim is being made in this "law." In spite of the fact that the two decisions are events that are distinct from the entry of the strongest reason, they may be expected always to follow if the mechanism is intact, not interfered with, and not overpowered by reflexes, accidents, and so forth. Under those conditions, in other words, if one truly wants something most of all in the physiological sense, then one will carry out some behavior to attain it. There is a mechanism or program running twenty-four hours a day that takes certain goals as input and produces behaviors as output. Given all of these other conditions, including the strength condition, to want most is to do. Physiologically under these common conditions, the reason that is the strongest does not merely impart a desirability characteristic. It goes further in being a sure sign that some behavior to satisfy the want part of the reason *will be undertaken*. In so saying, however, the relativity of the strength factor should not be neglected. With the mechanism operating perfectly and without interference, we may frequently want something very much and still not go after it, but that will always be because we want something else more, whether we are aware of this or not.

Strictly speaking, then, even true reasons are not causes, but we can go beyond this observation in two directions whenever the pertinent behavior has indeed taken place. First, we can note that true reasons are factual causes because a causal chain is involved, and the reason that is within the chain does indeed occupy a necessary slot in the physical causal scenario. Second, recognizing the reason and the two decisions as a rationally significant causal chain culminating in the physical cause of the behavior, we can capture the primary concepts involved parsimoniously by designating the true reason together with its two satellite decisions as the operative reason. Operative reasons, even if somewhat loosely speaking, are physical causes.

Neither the positive finding with regard to factual causation nor the negative finding with regard to reasons standing alone as physical causes is what is most important here for social research. The important finding is that the physiological and rational systems are so close in nature that events in the first are matched by concepts in the second—that we may describe the physiological mechanism so nearly and satisfactorily in psychological terms. The causal system that generates intentional behavior works very much like a rational system of wants, beliefs, goals, and decisions. It is no wonder that we find it so difficult to explain human behavior properly except by such entities as these. The behavior is in fact *caused* by such entities as these. They are not necessarily conscious and are not "under our control," but that does not detract from their validity as explainers. Operative reasons mean that there are "wants" and "beliefs" and "goals" inside of us relating to one another and acting in certain ways, and we intuitively know for certain that it is just such entities and relations as these that are responsible for what we do.

With these findings, the irregularity problem is solved. Given the role of the strength factor, we understand why neither aware nor unaware reasons are always causes. At the same time, we see by reference to the affect-object system that true reasons do indeed have a significant causal role and that operative reasons are physical causes of the pertinent behavior when it actually occurs. Nevertheless, because of the possibility of encounters with outside sources of interference, even the general category of operative reasons is not connected with behavior by universal laws.

Further, operative reasons show how we can repay the loan of intelligence (Dennett 1971); that is, we see how we get from the premises of a rational argument to the implementation of an intentional behavior by purely formal or mechanical means. The means-end procedure is a routine program that automatically selects from a "list" of relevant behaviors that might be performed when prompted by something in the role of "strongest want." Given that the means-end mechanism is operative, and in the absence of interfering encounters, a reason that satisfies the strength condition will always lead to the performance of some qualifying action.

Reasons, Thoughts, and Behavior

It remains for us to speculate on whether reasons and decisions in the form of thoughts were themselves causal whenever the pertinent behavior was in fact carried out. Research reported to date does not enable us to settle this issue. One obvious argument to the contrary, however, is that, because unaware operative reasons are frequently causal—as when the thought does not give the true reason or there is no relevant thought at all—and because the affect-object system is presumably operating full-time whether it is to some degree reflected in our thoughts or not, it seems highly unlikely that thoughts would suddenly and unnecessarily take over the causal role when they happen, outside of our control, to duplicate the elements of the operative reason. The thoughts in this perspective are superfluous.

But even if the thoughts are not causal, we do have them, and the appropriate behavior does often follow. Figure 1 presents two ways in which thoughts might be related to intentional behavior in case they themselves are not causal. First, thoughts might be perceptions of what is going on in the affect-object system. If so, they would be related to the behavior as collateral effects, as in figure 1a. The physiological mechanism would cause the conscious reason in the same sense as a chair causes our visual perception of the chair, and it would also of course cause the behavior. Note that if the relation actually were as portrayed in figure 1a, the conscious reasons and decisions would not be causes of the behavior—even factual causes. As collateral effects, some might claim that they were necessary and sufficient, but they would not occupy a necessary slot in the physical causal scenario.

One must consider the collateral effects relation to be somewhat dubious, however, because even a limited reflection of the physiological mechanism in our thoughts is highly erratic. Frequently, the reflection is quite incomplete, and there is no apparent explanation for this. It is as though our eyes were open and the chair were there, but we would see it about half the time and fail to see it the other half. There is another way, however, in which the same kind of relation between

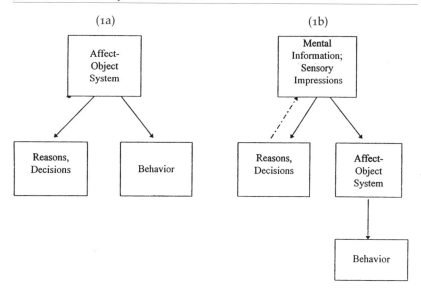

Fig. 1.   Relation of conscious reasons and decisions to behavior

thoughts and behavior might hold, but once removed. That is, thoughts may be related to behavior as collateral effects because they are also related to events in the affect-object system as collateral effects. The common cause in this case—and here we have a factual cause—would be the very sensory impressions and items from memory that populate the affect-object field (see fig. 1b—the dashed arrow will be discussed momentarily), only they would not work in the same way upon both systems. In this view, the system of conscious thought and the affect-object system apparently process much of the identical raw data but a bit differently, thus producing somewhat different products. As an analogy, consider the international news in the *New York Times* and the *Washington Post*. There is a great deal of similarity in the articles that appear in the two papers, but the results are far from identical. Because of differences in policies, procedures, and personnel, one is more inclusive than the other and wording and emphases vary. In much the same fashion, I suggest that the affect-object system is more inclusive than the relevant conscious processes and that objects and affect are portrayed within the two systems in subtly but importantly different ways. Yet, just as each newspaper captures a great deal of what is printed in the other, so too may conscious thoughts, without direct copying, capture much of what transpires in the affect-object system.

We saw earlier that thoughts are not causal in the sense that we can use them to control our behavior, and I might be taken now as suggesting that thoughts are never the causes of intentional behavior in any sense—never factual causes, that is, any more than physical. That is not entirely the case, however, as is indicated by the one reverse arrow in figure 1b. Conscious reasons and decisions are capable of influencing behavior by virtue of affect connected with those events *themselves*. That is, there are implications for behavior in liking to see oneself as being the sort of person who acts rationally (i.e., in terms of good reasons) or as one who has the "will power" to carry out decisions once made. All thinking is experience. The affect-object system monitors the consciousness just as it does the environment. The fact of having decided to do something or of recognizing that one has a good reason to do it is information that may be coupled with affect. If the pertinent behavior is carried out, the conscious reason or decision itself would have occupied a necessary slot and would have been a legitimate factual cause. Because I *decided* to go to the candidate reception, for example, that object may now become dominant and directive of my behavior. But of course it very well may not. Whether it does or not is not "a matter of choice" or a matter "subject to the will of the individual." What is determinative instead is the encounter of affects, where the strongest always wins. Nevertheless, conscious reasons and decisions may in this fashion play a frequent role in the determination of behavior, at least for some of us.

Conclusion

To the findings and conclusions on causation in chapters 1 and 2, I hope to have added in this chapter a demonstration (*a*) that aware reasons and decisions are not physical causes of intentional behavior in any meaningful sense but that operative reasons are, (*b*) that the dominance of a reason is determined by affect, (*c*) that the generation of intentional behavior depends on probabilistic encounters, chiefly, the encounter of any one reason active at a given time with others, and therefore (*d*) that strict laws or systematic generalizations concerning intentional human behavior are not possible (I leave the notion of probabilistic laws for chap. 5). We may now proceed to the examination of some specific implications of these several findings for social science research and theory.

Chapter 4

Design and Method

From the standpoint of the needs of social science, all of causation can-not be squeezed into one concept: there are two kinds of cause that are not congruent. Physical causation fails to recognize certain causal types. If we were successfully to disallow those types as causes, we would hamstring both social science discourse and ordinary thinking and communication. These include let-happen causes, encounters, and the causation of nonoccurrences, as we have seen, but also the explana-tion of many events that simply are not physical motions. In this last category, suppose one asked, for example, "What caused Yellowstone to become one of our most popular national parks?" This "becoming popular" is not, as it stands, the physical motion of anything. Yet we would like to explain it causally, and we do. Similarly, to say that Hamilton's ideas influenced "the Constitution," or that careful plan-ning by the chair caused the meeting to "run smoothly," or that demo-cratic supervision was responsible for "high morale," or that the approach of Christmas caused "heavy traffic" is to refer to effects that do not, as they stand, satisfy the definition given in chapter 2 of physi-cal causation. These statements of relationship that refer to empirical events but not necessarily to a physical relation between them are instances of factual causality. Physical and factual causation are thus fundamentally different from one another. Nonetheless, they are inti-mately related.

In spite of the fact that factual causality comes into use because of the narrow scope of physical causality and that its essence is distinct, physical causality nevertheless remains at its core. The concept of cause emanates fundamentally from the physical and no meaning of the term exists that ignores its physical roots. For that reason, there is a categor-ical difference between factual as well as physical causal relations on the one hand and logical relations of explanation or implication on the other. The idea of "cause" does not apply to the latter. We do not say, for example, that the distributive property causes three times eight to equal three times two plus three times six or that the rules of chess caused my opponent to be unable to capture my bishop with his knight or that the premises of a syllogism cause its conclusion (many similar examples may be found in Kim 1975). These relations are not ultimately physical, and therefore they are not ordinarily thought of as causal.

Factual cause is an explanatory device. As I noted earlier, one of its primary functions is to assign responsibility. We say, for example, that the going was slow because the print was small or that the reason the bridge collapsed was a rusted bolt or that in spite of the bad weather the approach of Christmas produced a hum of activity. It may be noted in passing that these examples of explanation are fairly bland. Factual cause, however, is frequently used in a much livelier sense as well, namely, to assign responsibility in such a way as to invoke moral judgment—praise, blame, fault, credit, guilt, commendation, and so forth: a difficult meeting ran smoothly owing to her superb organizational capacities; the inspector of last March 4 caused the eventual collapse of the bridge by being drunk on the job; it was her children who kept her spirits up in that difficult time.

Causal Reasoning

Social science uses both senses of causality, the physical and the factual. We try to explain behavior, and because behavior is physical, physical causality is inevitably at the root of the explanation. Yet the cause that we single out is often only a factual cause, as in Hamilton and the Constitution or the secretary of state's memo and the president's action. And even if it is a physical cause, as in the prestige motive and innovation or the desire for land and title and the decision to enter the tournament, it may be presented and argued for only as a factual cause. What I point to here is that there are two categories of causal reasoning in social science corresponding to the two types of causation. The kind of evidence that we bring to bear is different in the two cases. The reasoning and evidence in each category are what they are because they are designed to show that a certain proposed cause fulfills the requirements either of physical causation or of factual causation, and the two sets of requirements are quite distinct.

Factual causal reasoning is based on the idea of necessary slots. In this category, we would therefore generally reason by showing that X was necessary; that is, if not X then not Y. The reasoning would proceed as follows: Evidence is presented to show that Y occurred along with X (preferably having demonstrably followed X in time). This fulfills the part of the definition of factual causation that requires that "X and Y both occurred." In addition, not Y (or less Y, etc.) is shown to have gone along with not X (less X, etc.). This second aspect is what it takes in addition to establish the existence of a relationship in a correlational or survey design, and it also describes what happened in the control group in a standard randomized experiment. It is this aspect that provides an estimate of the counterfactual conditional that is critical to factual causation: assuming (often on a less secure basis than we would like) that the subjects in the not-X (or less-X) category were adequately similar to those in the X category, we can say on the basis of what happened to *them* that if not for X in the *others*, then not Y; X was necessary for Y in those subjects who were indeed characterized by both. It is important to keep in mind here that the basis of the method does not lie in the comparison of those characterized by X with those characterized by not-X. It lies rather in the comparison of those characterized by X with what would have occurred in the same group or individual had it been characterized by not-X instead, with the other group or individual involved serving merely as the basis for the estimation of this counterfactual. The latter role, however, is the most difficult and problematic. The crux of factual causal reasoning lies in presenting sound evidence for the counterfactual conditional—what *would have* happened if X had not been there.

Factual causal reasoning includes in particular (but is not limited to) all correlational argumentation, as in statistical designs. It also includes experimental and quasi-experimental designs, whether the analysis is statistical or not. It is in short the basis of ordinary quantitative research and of the stricture that we need comparison in order to establish causality, the comparison being between evidence for the co-occurrence of X and Y on the one hand and evidence for the counterfactual on the other. The relation between factual causal reasoning and these common types of quantitative analysis is so close that I will define "quantitative" research for present purposes simply as the type of research that rests on a comparison of these two kinds of evidence.

All physical causes are factual causes as well, but the reverse is not true. If the ball physically broke the window, then surely it occupied a necessary slot, but opening the shutter was *only* a factual cause in that it did not physically break the window. Factual causal reasoning is indispensable for establishing the causal status of factors that may be factual but not physical causes. Take health education research, for example. There we have statistical designs of various sorts in which the investigators conclude that knowing about certain risk factors leads to (i.e., causes) certain health-related behaviors, such as nutritionally sound eating habits (Edwards et al. 1985). There is no thought that this knowledge about risk factors might be a physical cause. Being exposed to information about proper nutrition, for example, is not thought to have *made* the subjects eat properly, but rather we can see that adequately motivated people (and it is in the motivation that the physical causation lies) are much more likely to eat properly if they have knowledge of what is proper than if they do not. The reasoning then proceeds by showing that those who received and absorbed the health education materials tended to eat properly. Those who did not, however, tended not to, thereby indicating that the knowledge in the first group occupied a necessary slot.

The entity X may in fact be a physical cause as well as a factual cause but if this particular reasoning process is used, X is thereby established only as a factual cause. In the nutrition field, for example, there are studies in which nutrition supplements were selectively provided to poor children in order to assess the relation between nutrition and cognitive development (McKay et al. 1980; Freeman et al. 1981). Because these designs were statistical, however, only factual causality was established; that is, it was determined that nutrition did indeed occupy a necessary slot, but whether it functioned in that slot like the ball (i.e., as a physical cause of cognitive development) or like the shutter (merely a factual cause) was not and could not be established by the design itself.

If there is a concern about redundancy or collateral effects (spuriousness), this ordinary counterfactual approach becomes inadequate. Necessary conditions must then be seen as different from necessary slots. For redundancy, there are two guidelines. One can establish X as a cause even though it may not itself have been strictly necessary if one can show that X was the factor that was physically there to perform a necessary function in the production of Y, as in the case of Hamilton and the Constitution. To do so, however, one clearly finds oneself filling in with physical reasoning, which we will come to in a moment. The second guideline warns against including two variables separately in an analysis if they fill the same functional slot—if they are fungible in a sense. As in the case of the student's own college and the parents' college when they are redundant determinants of income, each cause, when present, undermines the detectability of the other by indicating that in the counterfactual case, Y would have occurred anyway. The redundant causes might be alternative sources of the same resource or the same knowledge or alternative powerful motives for the same behavior. In all such cases, the presence of each cause in the absence of the other will show them both to have been unnecessary and yield the conclusion that, to some false degree, neither was causal. In regression analysis, for example, one causal coefficient or the other, or both, must inevitably be weakened, and this will be true regardless of whether the variables are entered additively or interactively. The antidote is to drop one, combine them in an index, or measure at a higher level of generality, such as "availability of financial means" or "knowledge of proper nutrition," regardless of the individual sources of the funds or the knowledge, respectively.

For collateral effects (and spuriousness), one might sometimes want to show that in spite of X's being a necessary condition, usually indicated by a notable correlation, it was not a cause of Y. In quantitative research this would almost invariably be attempted by controlling statistically for the presumed source of spuriousness and showing that the original correlation between X and Y then disappears (method A). Another possibility is to show by a physical analysis that there could be no causal connection between the two (method B). Thus, if the tobacco companies, for example, wish to demonstrate that cigarette smoking is generally not a cause of lung cancer (with co-occurrence by chance having been ruled out by significance tests) and wish to go beyond the meager defense that the link has not yet been proved conclusively, they must either produce statistically some sources of spuriousness that will make the relationship disappear (method A) or, by knowing both the etiology of the disease and the elements of cigarette smoking, show that there can be no possible physical causal link between the two (method B), just as there could have been none between James and John. More commonly, a correlation appears and the concern is to show that it is indeed causal and not spurious. Statistical tactics have a serious limitation. Several possible sources of spuriousness might be shown not to have had such effects, but there is always the possibility of spuriousness based in a variable that was not measured, and perhaps not even imagined. A physical analysis can hold more hope of a definitive determination. It is only necessary to show by a physical analysis that X was or even can be a physical cause of Y. This is precisely the task of those who would demonstrate that the statistical link between cigarette smoking and lung cancer is causal and not spurious.

Physical causal reasoning is entirely different. There are no hypotheticals or counterfactual conditionals involved, such as "if not X"; no comparison is necessary. Physical causation has to do with a force and a motion, and physical causal reasoning proceeds by showing that it was indeed force X that produced motion Y. Many have suggested to me at this point in the argument that physical causal reasoning is at bottom counterfactual reasoning—that we know the motion was the effect of the force because we know that if the force had not impinged on the object, the motion would not have occurred. This position is highly problematic. First of all, the traditional counterfactual is not always true when X is a cause, and when the counterfactual is not true we can often detect the causation anyway. Counterfactual reasoning in those instances therefore cannot be the source of the correct causal inference. The case of Annie and Manny shows this conclusively; that is, we know that Manny was the cause of Annie's jumping even though the counterfactual statement that "if Manny had not yelled Annie would not have jumped" is patently false. She would in fact have jumped anyway. Those who want to see a counterfactual behind every causal inference should recognize here that, in spite of the fact that there is no way we could have been properly informed by the pertinent counterfactual reasoning—and in fact would have been completely misled by it—we were unquestionably able to come to the correct causal conclusion anyway. Furthermore, there is a reason that we were able to do so, and this reason should be confronted; it should not be ignored for convenience. Second, the counterfactual way often is simply not the way we reason, even when, as is usually the case, the counterfactual happens to be true. Suppose you stub your toe and cry out and sit down to hold it, and I say, "Why are you holding your foot?" and you say, "Because I stubbed my bare toe," and I then say, "How do you know it is because of that?" You would not say, "Because I know that if I hadn't stubbed my toe I would not be sitting down and holding it." It may be true that you would not be holding it—and then again there is some possibility that it actually is not true—but in any case that was not your reasoning process. You never stopped to think about that; it is not the way you arrived at your knowledge of why you are now nursing your toe. You arrived at your knowledge by recognizing certain feelings and desires: you felt a searing pain coming from the region of your toe as it encountered the iron leg of the bed and subsequently felt the desire to hold it because, for the moment, it *hurt*! To deny this is to risk being caught in a certain fanaticism or dogmatism, whereas to accept it is to begin to broaden the issue of causation in a potentially productive direction.

How about physical causal reasoning in regard to human behavior? If we accept the affect-object paradigm, then in the case of intentional human behavior the physical force is contained in the physiological entities that comprise the operative reason. The point of physical causal reasoning is then to illuminate this relation between force and motion, that is, between operative reason and behavior. First, we must show that the person or group studied did indeed have the reason to which we want to attribute causality. Second, we need to make the case that this reason was very strong relative to other considerations that could have been active at the time. Third, it is generally crucial to show by various other manifestations that it was indeed this reason that was operating—tracing out the "signature" of the reason in the modus operandi approach that I will describe in the following section. Fourth, in some instances, it is important to rule out other reasons by showing that their active prevalence would have produced certain signs that were not in fact observed. And last, we often need to establish that it is proper to interpret the actors' behavior as innovation or preventive health measures or whatever it is that we now want to call it. The discipline of history is full of physical causal reasoning. We are shown, for example, why William Marshal and other well-born men in the Middle Ages participated in tournaments and jousts. They wanted very much to obtain patronage or to marry heiresses or in some other way to acquire land and titles, and, not being eldest sons, few other routes to these benefits were open to them (Duby 1985). Note that a statistical study might well have proceeded in part by showing that the great majority of participants in such contests were second sons, illegitimate sons, sons of ruined fathers, and so on, and that only a very small minority of contestants were eldest sons or individuals who otherwise stood to inherit under primogeniture. This is not, however, the manner in which Duby proceeds. He has no such data. He proceeds by making us feel, or see clearly and vividly, the life position and therefore the operative reasons characteristic of the kinds of individuals who did participate in jousts and tournaments—William Marshal being perhaps an archetype both in motivation and success.

Physical causal reasoning is common in the social science disciplines outside of history as well. Consider as one example Barley's (1990) study of the relation between technology and structure in hospitals. Whereas most prior research on this topic has been statistical, relating measures of the complexity of technologies to the decentralization of structures, Barley sought to show just *how* structure might be affected by technology. In showing how and why changes in technology affected certain particular behaviors of individuals by which we measure "structure," he highlighted physical rather than factual causal reasoning. Technological advances in diagnostic radiological equipment far beyond the ordinary X-ray led to the training of technicians who could understand and operate this equipment and the hiring of such technicians by the hospitals studied. Because older physicians needed to communicate with their patients and make medical decisions based on these diagnostic outcomes, they consulted with and depended upon the new technicians for interpretations and even medical advice—something they had never done with the ordinary X-ray technicians—and this new pattern of decentralized interaction constituted an important part of the structural change observed. What Barley has shown us with this story or account are the *reasons* and the *strength* of the reasons behind behaviors that amounted to structural change. Thus, even though Barley does incorporate some sophisticated statistical techniques in his article, even though he makes before-after comparisons, and even though his takeoff point is aggregate sociological *variables* (organizational technology and organizational structure), still, his design—that is, the basis of his causal conclusions—is an in-depth study of radiology units in two hospitals, both of which exhibited the behavior pattern just recounted. His core reasoning is physical causal reasoning.

We can also begin to see from Barley's study that explaining behavior by reasons is indeed a prominent approach in social science, even though this might not always or even often be explicit. The theoretical focus of his paper, technology and structure, seems on the surface to have very little to do either with reasons or behavior. Clearly, however, structure is a matter of behaviors, and a moment's thought shows that the same is true of a great many other constructs in social science that might not seem at first glance to be a matter of behaviors at all, such as power, budgets, democracy, segregation, the level of development of countries, and so forth. Even if these concepts are behavioral at bottom, we may not seek to explain such behavior explicitly by reasons. We may have good cause to want to operate at a level of aggregation or abstraction above that of the individual person, for example, as we do when we explain structure by "technology." Reasons, however, must be at the bottom of it somewhere. This emerges occasionally when the reason that is tacitly *assumed* to underpin a hypothesis is challenged. In this very area of technology and structure, for example, Child (1972) pointed out that the basic hypothesis assumes that executives will act so as to try to make their units more effective (i.e., structure is manipulated to suit new technologies in order to maintain effectiveness, so that effectiveness would be the operative reason), whereas in truth, Child urged, executives under such changing circumstances will often make "strategic choices" by which effectiveness might be sacrificed to any of a number of other desiderata and constraints. In Barley's study, effectiveness (in patient care) may well have been a relatively minor concern, but if it was then another operative reason still produced a causal link between technology and structure. Although he is not as searching as he might have been had he been trying self-consciously to establish the operative reasons, his account makes it clear that the older physicians were largely motivated by the face-saving need to appear informed and up to date in their contacts with younger colleagues and with patients. Stinchcombe has based almost an entire book on this relation between aggregate or abstract concepts (such as "technology") on the one hand and individual reasons on the other, and he puts the general case well (Stinchcombe 1990: 19): "Since, of course, all the significant organizational acts that we will be explaining are done on purpose by conscious individuals, any explanation at the social level has ultimately to be shown to be adequate at the level of intentions of individuals. . . . If in fact individuals make up functional structures, this is surely an important dependent phenomenon that people who specialize in explaining individual behavior ought to address. This individual-level explanation is God's work, but not my own particular vocation." Wanting to produce theory at the aggregate level—in fact his subject is the relation between information needs and organizational structure—but wishing to show also that the explanations are "adequate at the level of intentions of individuals," Stinch-combe is led inexorably to in-depth analyses that are clearly exercises in physical causal reasoning.

There can be no question but that social scientists make important contributions working at a variety of levels of aggregation and abstraction, but I would urge that getting down to individuals and intentions, even if only as a matter of sensitivity to that level of explanation, will frequently be highly informative.

Last, it is not only possible but often highly desirable to mix the two forms of reasoning in the same study and even in the demonstration of the same point. The two proliferate in social science in healthy integration, although the mixture is not often noticed. Suppose one evaluated one or more seat belt laws to explore whether such laws save lives and serious injuries by increasing seat belt use (Lee 1986). Factual causal reasoning shows a statistical relation between the seat belt laws and both increased usage rates and decreased death rates, with "before" measures used to estimate the counterfactuals. For the causal link between seat belt use and mortality and injury in accidents, however, we rely in part on evidence from actual staged crashes using elaborately wired crash dummies—a process of physical causal reasoning.

Causation and the Case Study

I want to suggest that the way in which we think about causation in social research may be flawed. Amending the current view could result in a different everyday perspective on research design in the social disciplines, a perspective that would make causal inference more accessible and that would not tie it exclusively to the comparative method, even in research that is primarily quantitative. We have seen repeatedly that attempts to conceptualize causation are plagued by question begging. We find again and again that we use an undercover definition of causality both in normal communication and in the process of forging and judging explicit definitions, the underlying or naive view being, I would claim, our sense of physical or mechanical connection and of forces. The basis of revamping the current view is to allow physical causation to become part of it, in accord with the analysis of the first two chapters of this book. In addition, but not so obviously, the pertinence of the new view is extended to large areas of human science through the recognition that operative reasons are physical causes, as we saw in chapter 3. An analysis of the case study as a research design illuminates these issues.

The ordinary explanatory research project in the social sciences has a dual aim: (*a*) we try through our research to explain behavior as it occurs in certain observed instances, and (*b*) we try also to make this explanation broadly applicable, that is, valid for enough similar but unobserved instances to justify the effort as a genuine contribution to knowledge rather than as a bit of gossip. In evaluation research, this dual aim is roughly paralleled by the concerns for "internal" and "external" validity. Internal validity raises the issue of whether the treatment caused the outcome in the subjects and setting observed, whereas external validity raises the issue of generalizability to subjects and settings that were not observed (see Campbell and Stanley 1966).

I will now refer to and indeed define a case study in part as a design based on a "sample of one." By this I do not mean that only one observation is made. On the contrary, the typical case study includes hundreds of observations. I use this terminology to highlight the case study in its capacity as a research design, that is, a method of establishing internal and external validity—causality and generalizability. I wish to establish the pure form of a category that is distinct from what I referred to above as a quantitative research design—one based on factual causal reasoning, crucially featuring evidence *both* that X and Y occurred and also that the counterfactual—if not X then not Y—is probably true. The second or alternative category of design would be one in which we empirically observe that X and Y occurred, but, in order to make the inference of a causal relation between the two, we do not use evidence for the counterfactual. There is only one *kind* of case, in other words, even though there might be several examples of it, for example, the kind of case in which the new technology *was* being used and the structure *was* decentralized. I will refer to a prominent subtype of this second category as the case study, and I will also assume for purposes of the present discussion that only one unit of the kind being observed—one hospital, seat belt law, country, and so on—is included (more than one would make it a type of small-n study, which I will also explore). Still, hundreds of observations on the one hospital or country and its relevant environment would be made, but at the core of any causal inference in the study, as for example the inference that technology affected structure, there would be one unit with one score on X (e.g., advanced technology) and one on Y (e.g., decentralized structure—see Eckstein 1975 for a similar definition of a case study). I recognize that many studies commonly referred to as "case studies" are not of this variety, but I suggest that in the matter of research design it is instructive and not inapt to apply this label. It does capture much of the essence of an important distinction, and the distinction is one that does frequently implicate "case studies" in a critical way, even as more broadly conceived (see, for example, Achen and Snidal 1989).

The case study—research using a sample of only one but that one treated in substantial depth and detail—is commonly considered to be inferior to large-sample research in terms of both internal and external validity. If your research on a developing country finds that the country is doing remarkably well under young, dynamic leadership, and if you wish to attribute the performance of the country at least in part to the nature of the leadership, it would commonly be considered that you were on shaky ground. Many would even say that your explanatory aim was impossible given your research design—the case study. This view rests on the tenet that variance on the explanatory variable is required to establish causality. In your case, the only leadership you observed was young and dynamic. What would have happened if the leadership had been old and stodgy? We do not know because you have not made any observations of that sort. Perhaps exactly the same performance would have been achieved, in which case we certainly would not attribute the observed outcome to youth and dynamism.

Even if we believed your explanatory inference about leadership in the observed country, the value of your research would still be questionable—now on grounds of external validity or generalizability. How can we have any confidence that your findings are broadly applicable? Your sample is a sample of one and may therefore be quite unrepresentative of other countries to which we might want to be able to apply the insights you obtained. Your findings may indeed be unique, in which case they would be essentially worthless for social science.

I want to suggest, however, that these conceptions of the limitations of the case study as a research design are superficial and overdrawn. It is extremely important in this connection to see that we have no designs at all in social science that will accomplish the dual aim of research mentioned above with a high degree of assurance and reliability. All designs have quite serious limitations with respect to either one goal or the other. I will advance the view that when the extent of these limitations is recognized and we speak relatively, the case study is potentially an excellent vehicle for advancing both of the general goals and should not *in principle* occupy an inferior position to large- or small-sample research of any description. I emphasize "in principle" because much depends on whether the case study design, and indeed any design, is applied well or poorly and is a good fit for the possibilities and requirements of the research questions at issue in a particular project.

Case Studies and the Dual Aim of Research

In a previous publication (Mohr 1985), I tried to support the claim in the preceding paragraph with respect to both internal and external validity. The case with regard to external validity seems to me still to be strong, and I will characterize it briefly here. The case originally made with regard to internal validity, however, was specialized to a certain type of case study that is not common in social research and, even for that type, there was a weakness lurking beneath the surface of the argument. I will now try to strengthen the argument with respect to internal validity based on the findings of earlier chapters.

External validity. The best route to external validity in science is to be able to hold the "homogeneity assumption" (see "unit homogeneity" in Holland 1986 and the "auxiliary assumption" in Mohr 1985). This is an assumption that "all subjects or cases in the same class as the subjects actually studied (people, organizations, rocks, rivers, innovations, etc.) are equivalent on dimensions or characteristics that would affect the inference at stake. . . . For some purposes, not only is a rose a rose, but a hunk of iron is a hunk of iron, and a falling body is a falling body" (Mohr 1985: 72–73).

This assumption is commonly made without hesitation or objection in much of physics and in some areas of biology, but it is hardly tenable in the explanation of intentional human behavior. We cannot just assume that all people and groups will react to certain social, psychological, or environmental forces in the same way nor even special subclasses of people, such as women, small groups, formal organizations, and so forth. If we could do this with any frequency, the case study would be our primary research design. As it stands, we are not able to do behavioral research on a single individual or on a specific group and assume at the same time that the results will be valid for all others, or even for all others of a certain sort, such as Americans, tall

Americans, children, or voluntary associations. What this means is that in the main, if not entirely, case studies of human behavior cannot be made the basis for systematic generalization, even within a subclass. Exactly the same, however, is true of large-sample research. No sample and no population can be made to stand for all of humanity or even all within a given class.

Without benefit of the homogeneity assumption, there are three routes to a limited but still potentially valuable generalizability commonly available in social science: (*a*) probability sampling, (*b*) replication, and (*c*) understanding the process. The first, probability sampling, is a large-sample affair. For statistical reasons, a random sample or other probability sample must be greater than one—not a case study, in other words—and in general should be, say, twenty-five or more in order to be efficacious. Here, large-sample research would seem to have the edge over the case study, and indeed it does but with three caveats: (*a*) the sample must indeed be based on random selection, (*b*) one can generalize on this basis only to the population sampled, and (*c*) even for that population, the time period that technically appertains to the generalization is the past time period, the one in which the sample was observed, and not any future time period. Although this approach does give large-sample research an edge, the caveats mean that it is a narrow edge. The first caveat narrows the scope of application of this advantage considerably, but it is to the second and third that attention should be drawn in particular. Probability sampling does not in itself convey an advantage in producing theories of human behavior; it only allows one to generalize to a certain confined subset of humanity, such as the electorate of the United States of America or the New York Public Schools or those admitted to the county hospital in June, and even then only to that subset as it was when the sample was drawn. In many ways, therefore, each such subset in itself simply represents a case for study.

The second and third approaches, replication versus understanding the process, are the classic opposing positions on this question of large-sample research versus the case study—replication supposedly favoring large-sample research and understanding favoring the case study. With respect to large-sample research, replication can mean two things: administering the research protocol to several individuals (or groups)—such that the number of replications is essentially a synonym for the size of the sample—or doing the research all over again on one or more additional large samples.

Taking replication as a synonym for sample size, we might conclude from a research project that X apparently caused Y (or some similar form of explanatory statement) in, say, 40 percent of the group studied. For example, we might find that the difference in the proportion satisfied with their jobs among those who did and did not participate extensively in decision making was .4—60 percent satisfied in the participating group and 20 percent among those who did not participate. It is difficult to see the replication here either as permitting a general statement in itself or as a good basis for generalizing to other individuals or groups. It does not permit a general statement in itself to the effect that "participation apparently causes job satisfaction" because, although far more than one person who participated was indeed satisfied, many (40 percent) in the participating group were not satisfied, while some (20 percent) of their counterparts who did not participate were satisfied. The most favorable conjecture we might make is that participation *sometimes* causes satisfaction, recognizing that often (and we do not know just when) it does not. That is not necessarily much better than the statement one might make by studying a single individual who was more satisfied after participation was introduced than he or she was before. Moreover, we would not feel we should predict that the difference of proportions in another study group or population or time period would also take the particular value of .4. We have learned from experience, in fact, that it is highly likely to be either more than .4 or less, and often considerably more or less, depending on the group studied.

If we take replication to mean repeating the study in another large sample, this same sort of experience tells us that the method will not provide a basis for generalization. There will be variation in outcomes from one study population to another, and that variation will leave us not knowing what quantity might be the true theoretical one, if such a quantity exists. We can replicate the studies, in other words, but we do not seem to be able to replicate the results, at least not very widely. Rogers and Shoemaker (1971: 346–85), for example, reviewed hundreds of studies of predictors of innovation and showed a substantial spread of results on each predictor variable—sometimes even ranging from significantly positive as a predictor to significantly negative. Given that innovative behavior is governed by encounters, this result is unsurprising in principle. What many of us seem to hope for is that, *in practice,* we will nevertheless find predictors so endowed with affect and associations that they win out in almost every actual encounter, probabilistic as that may be. Here is where the experience of social science rather than principle is the guide. Unfortunately, our experience with discovering good, strong, important, and broadly applicable cause-and-effect relations is negative—we have not made any such discoveries. I suggest that if we very carefully think about each predictor of each outcome in which we have a research interest, we will conclude that the chances of its turning out to be such a universal winner in the battle of the affect-object dyads are slim. In sum, replication does not seem to be a reliable basis of generalization in social science. If the case study found a better basis in the method of understanding the process, it would come out ahead.

It is in fact common to feel that understanding the background of a certain behavior in depth teaches something valuable in terms of future conduct. That kind of generalization is, after all, presumably an important reason behind our interest in history, as well as in great novels. Unfortunately, however, no one then takes a rigorous look to see just how much has really been taught by such works. Perhaps it is not possible to measure just how valid the tacit generalization from a historical or other case study truly is. It may well be that the quality of learning from such insightfully rendered vicarious experience is not overwhelmingly high. Nevertheless, most would agree that we would not be willing to give the method up as a part of ordinary life—we feel that we learn from stories about others. Many would also agree, even if they did not consider a good history or case study to be "science," that there is something to be learned from such research products in terms of behavioral expectations in similar circumstances. When we know enough of just the right facts about a situation to be able to empathize with, or quite thoroughly understand, the behavior of the actors, we feel that the information we tuck away has a good chance of being reused with profit at some future time. This describes a process of creative-selective generalization. Generalizability of this sort from the case study is indefinite, but it does seem to be possible, and this creative-selective sort is, I suggest, the best kind of generalization we can have in social science, aside from the limited type that is permitted by probability sampling. I will treat the topic at somewhat greater length in chapter 5.

In external validity, then, there does not seem to be a substantial advantage in large-sample research. In fact, it may be the other way around.

Internal validity. With respect to internal validity, the potential problem with case studies inheres not in the possible unrepresentativeness of a sample of one but in the lack of variance on explanatory variables. In large-sample research, such variance enters by way of the empirical observation of individuals with varying scores on X as a basis both for documenting the co-occurrence of X and Y and for estimating the counterfactual—participating and not participating in decision making, for example, or various levels of technology or age and stodginess of the leadership. Clearly then, there can be absolutely no variance on X in the case study. If the sample truly is a sample of one in the sense specified earlier, then each causal variable may by definition be represented in the research by only one score.

In an earlier publication on this subject (Mohr 1985), I supported the potential internal validity of case studies in two ways, the first being to point out that one can build the necessary contrasts into the case study itself. In particular, one can study a single individual or group over time so that, for example, performance of the country after the accession of a young, dynamic leader might be contrasted with its performance before that time. As we have defined the case study here, however, such a device amounts to cheating. We would really be talking about a sample of two or more in such instances and would therefore not be talking about the pure form of the case study. It might be argued that almost all real-life case studies make this sort of comparison, that case studies are not so limited that they cannot contrast later observations with earlier ones or perhaps contrast unusual behavior actually studied with behavior that is known to be common or standard. Let us not, however, confuse "real-life" case studies with the case study as a research design, which requires a sample of one. If we do, we will gain little because we are likely to stay rooted in counterfactual views of causality. I would like to show that, remaining technically faithful to the definition, the case study as a design also may function to establish causation. The kinds of comparisons often built into "real-life" case studies will be covered in the section on small-sample designs later in this chapter.

In my earlier paper, the other base of support for the potential internal validity of case studies was the example of the modus operandi approach to causation, as discussed several times by Scriven (1966: 250; 1976):

Its basis lies in the recognition that when X causes Y it may operate so as to leave a "signature," or traces of itself that are diagnostic. In other words, one can tell when it was X that caused Y, because certain other things that happened and are observed unequivocally point to X. At the same time, one knows the signature of other possible causes of Y and one may observe that those traces did *not* occur. By using this technique, one often can make a strong inference that X either did or did not cause Y in a certain case. For the present purpose, moreover, one notes in passing the affinity of this approach for the study of a single case. The kind of example of the modus operandi approach that is frequently given reminds one of the work of a detective or a diagnostician. This approach might be used, for example, to determine the cause of death when several possibilities exist, such as a heart attack before the crash or a concussion afterwards, or it might be used to determine the cause of the overheating of a car engine. (Mohr 1985: 82–83)

One problem with reliance on the modus operandi approach for internal validity in case studies is that we do not seem to have many opportunities to use it. No doubt historical research does contain many applications. Collingwood (1946: 249–82), for example, advocates what is essentially this general approach as a basic method of sound historical inquiry. One is hard pressed, however, to find good examples in the other social disciplines. It does not seem to fit the needs of demonstration in the kinds of case studies commonly undertaken. For example, when Perrow (1963) tries to show that the medical staff was able to take power away from the trustees of a hospital because of the large scale of important technical advances in medicine at the time it would have been overly belaboring a quite acceptable point to think of all other possible causes of the change in power relations and show that their signatures were not to be found. It was enough to show the evidence that technical medical issues were becoming crucial in the operations of the hospital and that whereas the doctors could deal with them, the trustees could not. Thus, if the only route to the internal validity of case studies were the modus operandi approach, intriguing as it may be, one would have to conclude that, outside of history, relatively few case studies in social science have been or will be able to boast of strong internal validity.

A second problem with the rescue by modus operandi is more

philosophical. By what miracle can this method demonstrate causality if the critical ingredient of variance on the causal variable is lacking? Surely, neither the regularity theory nor factual causation is adequate since both require comparison with a counterfactual. We do teach in methods courses that correlation does not prove causation, but this is in the context of the dictum that it is, however, a minimal requirement (e.g., Selltiz et al. 1976). That is why the criticism of the case study seems so devastating: there *is* no way of establishing causality except via comparison with an estimate of the counterfactual. If you did not study old and stodgy, then you simply cannot attribute causality to young and dynamic. Modus operandi, however, appears to proceed by some different route. Only one instance is observed—one death in a car crash, for example. True, we may know from prior experience or research that heart attacks can cause both deaths and car crashes, and this knowledge may be important to us in some cases, but even then the prior experience or research may well not have used the regularity theory or factual causality to reach its conclusion and, in any case, neither is being used to determine whether a heart attack was indeed causal in this instance. The investigator does not explicitly consider crashes in which there was a heart attack and no heart attack, a death and no death. He or she simply looks for traces of a heart attack in the one case at hand. The whole idea of *variables* among which a correlation might be established seems irrelevant to this method. Is the modus operandi approach therefore weak as a basis of internal validity, or is there some elaboration of the idea of causation that shows it to be strong?

I suggest that it is strong and that it is physical causal reasoning that makes it so. Moreover, when we accept that operative reasons are physical causes, the essence of the modus operandi method is shown not only to be relevant to social science in principle but to be extendable in practice to that large proportion of social science whose goal is the explanation of the intentional behavior of individuals and groups. Last, we are able to see that physical causal reasoning makes causal inference available to the case study in general and not only to that variety of case study that employs the full modus operandi method.

Causal Reasoning, Internal Validity, and the Case Study

The modus operandi method seems at once strange and natural as a way of demonstrating causality. The strangeness has to do with the absence of variables, correlations, and counterfactuals—our usual formal props when the issue of causation is raised. These elements, however, make up only one of the two possible forms of causal reasoning. The other is physical causal reasoning, and that clearly is the basis of the modus operandi design. The method is a familiar part of life. By chains of physical causal reasoning, the detective, the physician, the cause-of-death coder, and the garage mechanic establish that X_1 meets all the requirements—all of the instances of physical causation that make up its "signature" have taken place—whereas X_2 through X_k fail to recommend themselves as causes by this test.

Thus, the view of causation elaborated in chapter 2 shows how the modus operandi method can establish causation, but at the same time the fact that we readily accept causation by the modus operandi method shows that we do also readily accept physical causation as causation. We do not need variables, correlations, and counterfactuals (not to mention that these cannot stand alone as a definition).

In social science, the physical causes of intentional behavior are operative reasons. It is plain that physical causal reasoning may be a persuasive method for establishing causation, and because, by way of operative reasons, that form of reasoning may clearly be executed through case studies of human behavior, the case study—research using a sample of only one but that one treated in substantial depth and detail—is a design that is not only pertinent but well suited to establishing causality in social science. We look in all possible ways for the signature of the proposed operative reason. As noted above, the execution of the task would involve making a convincing case that the person or group studied did indeed have the reason to which we want to attribute causality, that related actions and inactions reflect the pursuit of this goal, and that this reason, in context, was so strong relative to other considerations possibly active at the time that we understand how it overpowered the reasons for carrying out other actions and other reasons for the same action. It may also be important to establish that the effects—the actions we wish to interpret as innovation, preventive health behavior, or whatever—are properly interpreted. Finally, in some instances it may help a great deal to rule out other reasons as causes by showing that the pursuit of those would have produced certain signs that were not in fact observed—that these other signatures were not manifest. (See King et al. 1994 for whom this kind of reasoning on signatures is important in the absence of large samples, although they do not take up the fact that another definition of causality is apparently involved.)

It will be pointed out that, although we might be able to make a pretty good case in this fashion on the basis of physical causal reasoning, we cannot make an airtight one. There might well be doubt whether the reason supported as causal in a piece of research was indeed the operative reason. This reservation is valid and important but not damaging. The difficulty is relative; other approaches have similar problems. In particular, one cannot make an airtight case on the basis of factual causal reasoning either. In survey and quasi-experimental designs, the threats of spuriousness and other forms of "selection bias" can never be extinguished altogether, making the dictum that "correlation does not equal causation" a very serious and salient caveat (Mohr 1995: 169–70). In randomized experiments, the threat of "contamination" is similarly persistent, as is also the reservation that the statistical causal inference carries a probability of error equal to the significance level: we *will* make errors about 5 percent of the time. On the positive side, we sometimes have substantial confidence that the case made for a physical cause is valid, just as we have a great deal of confidence at times, although certainly not all of the time, in the conclusions of factual causal reasoning.

The true criticism of the case study, therefore, is not that it is a design by which it is difficult to establish causality but that it is a design by which it is difficult to establish causality through factual causal reasoning. How serious a criticism is this? Is factual causal reasoning somehow better, at least for social science? In effect, is it not better to have a *correlation* from which to theorize than to have but one causal instance? The question is clearly a very pertinent one, for faith in correlations and experiments in contrast to case studies will be hard to shake, but addressing it demands recognizing in the first instance that this issue of what is better is a question about *general theory*, about *external* rather than internal validity. Operative reasons *are* causes, and a particular one *was* a cause in this instance. The only question that can remain is, how general is this relation? Whereas factual causal reasoning can show the reasons of many individuals (implicitly or explicitly), physical causal reasoning will generally show the reasons only of one or a few. Is this a significant distinction? After touching one last base in the area of research design, I address that question in the following chapter.

In sum, it is difficult to do highly valuable theoretical research in social science primarily because the homogeneity assumption is generally untenable, and external validity is therefore elusive. Internal validity has received much more attention, but it is not nearly so formidable a challenge. In particular, it may be achieved by means of physical as well as factual causal reasoning.

Small-Sample Designs

In closing this chapter, let us turn to the question of small-sample research and examine its status as a design in light of the above analysis both of case studies and of studies based on large samples. By "small-n" or "small-sample," we usually mean research closely resembling the case study in approach but considering several units of analysis—programs, organizations, decisions, countries, and so forth—instead of only one. The idea of "small" in this context is not well defined, but it is best to think in terms of samples of two to four since larger numbers begin to make the deep and intensive analysis characteristic of the case study approach unwieldy. Given that the designs on either side of the small-n study can be valid bases for causal inference, it would seem that the same must be true for the category in the middle. However, that is not readily seen to be the case.

Considered as a would-be large-sample design oriented around factual causal reasoning, the paucity of subjects becomes, in principle at least, a serious shortcoming. The problems, which are well known in quantitative research, have to do with spuriousness, chance, and degrees of freedom. First, two units might differ both in X and Y, but we cannot infer a causal relation between those variables because the units might also differ on some third variable that causes their scores on both X and Y—the problem known as spuriousness or as a form of specification error due to omitted variables (see the discussion of collateral effects in chapter 1). We might find in our analysis of city A, for example, that rising expenditures for police were accompanied over a period of a few years by a falling crime rate and at the same time in city B that stagnant expenditures were accompanied by a rising crime rate. Is the relation between expenditures and crime rate causal? Perhaps not. Rising employment in city A may have caused both the increased expenditures and the reduced crime rate, while persistent unemployment in city B was causing both stagnant expenditures and a rising crime rate. The apparent causal connection between expenditures (X) and crime rate (Y) would in that case be spurious. Second, two units might differ in Y because of some factor that did *not* also cause their difference in X but just happened by what is variously referred to as chance or coincidence or sampling error to covary with X in this research. For example, school district A voted about three years ago to decentralize most academic decision making to individual school principals, whereas school district B has remained centralized. In the most recent round of standardized testing, district A gained significantly more than district B over the baseline averages of three years back. Was decentralization the cause of the greater gain? Perhaps not. Two medium-sized private organizations from out of state relocated to district A about three years ago, and several smaller organizations left, while there was almost no economic turnover in district B. Whereas the turnover in families had no impact on the decision to decentralize, let us say, the new children were on the average smarter or better trained than the old, thus raising standardized test scores. In this study, decentralization (X) was related to achievement (Y) by chance.

If the number of subjects studied is large, we can detect whether salient possible sources of spuriousness (unemployment, etc.) are indeed acting in that manner by bringing them into the analysis as control variables. With a very small number of subjects (e.g., cities), however, this common device is rendered almost completely useless. Given that the number of independent subjects observed must exceed the total number of variables, the analysis of spuriousness quickly becomes impossible as the addition of control variables eats up the required "degrees of freedom." Similarly, if the number of subjects studied is large, we can hope to rule out chance relations by another technique, the test of statistical significance. Unfortunately, this common device is also rendered essentially useless in small-sample research because almost no relationship will be statistically significant with a sample size of two to four.

The great bulk of prior social science scholarship on small-n designs strains against these difficulties (Lijphart 1971; Geddes 1990; Collier 1991). That is, the literature tends overwhelmingly to see small-n designs as *quantitative studies with special problems* and to ponder how to mitigate those problems. The tendency is understandable because large-n research and factual causal reasoning have been considered paradigmatic in terms of design. Most recently, King, Keohane, and

Verba (1994) have written an excellent book on the constructive use of quantitative reasoning in small-n research. Their approach and method can help a great deal to strengthen inferences from such designs and to avoid nonobvious pitfalls, and the same may be said for suggestions in the three other works just cited. There is nevertheless a highly salient danger—rooted in spuriousness, chance, and degrees of freedom—that is irreducible in principle. Taken as a design that depends on factual causal reasoning, the small-n study is inherently deficient in a critical component: the number of units of analysis is generally too small to permit the confident fulfillment of one indispensable requirement for reaching the causal conclusion either under the definition of factual causation or the traditional counterfactual definition. In factual causation, this requirement is that "X occupied a necessary slot *in the physical causal scenario* pertinent to Y." When there are so few total units of analysis, it is too difficult to know that the physical causal scenario in the contrasting or "control" cases was adequately comparable; that is, the few units that were used to cover the case in which X was not present may lead to spurious or chance relationships because they were dissimilar in critical ways from the first units. To take a final example, let us suppose that in country A the socialists refused to allow the communist party into the ruling coalition following a revolution, and a long period of stability ensued. In country B, the communists did join the coalition, and the revolution was reversed soon afterward by a right-wing coup d'etat. It is highly problematic on this basis to sustain the hypothesis that left-wing fragmentation caused stability following the revolution in country A because the scenario pertinent to stability there may not have been duplicated very well in country B. There may have been another relevant difference between country A and country B, so that it is difficult to tell whether fragmentation occupied a necessary slot. To rule out spuriousness and chance owing to such differences in scenario, a larger study population—more degrees of freedom—would generally be required.

Using the concepts of the counterfactual definition, the similar requirement is that "*in the circumstances,* if not X then not Y," which refers essentially to the same difficult to specify but critical elements as "the physical causal scenario."

As noted, King, Keohane, and Verba (1994) urge the application of various sound procedures that have primarily been associated with quantitative research, such as avoiding selection bias. For the most part, these involve considering X and Y to be *variables,* maintaining an orientation toward factual causal reasoning and the counterfactual definition—the preferred definition of causation in their work. I would reemphasize that this is a highly risky strategy for small-n researchers. The shortage of numbers is a grave liability that is unlikely to be overcome by the whole battery of suggested measures. In particular, the challenges of spuriousness and chance relations may easily persist in spite of these best efforts and if they do, and if one remains wedded to the counterfactual paradigm, then there is little recourse and it is hard to avoid the feeling that one is simply stuck in a second-class category of research.

One measure emphasized by King, Keohane, and Verba does not depend on considering X and Y to be variables, namely, looking for and checking out the *implications* of a correct inference, that is, changes or states in the world we should expect to observe if our inference that X caused Y is valid. As noted in our discussion of the case study, this is close to the idea of researching a signature in the modus operandi method. The procedure is always a good one but, except in one form, it is not reliably available in social science. It is more available when laws of nature are at issue, which might easily have implications for a variety of events in the world. It is hard, however, to think what other observations should be predicted given the inference that increased expenditures caused a drop in the crime rate in city A, or the inference that decentralization caused higher test scores, or that fragmentation caused stability. If it were a question whether X were there at all, such as whether the accident victim had had a heart attack, then other effects of X should perhaps have occurred and we could check for these, but in a great deal of social science research (not all, to be sure) we know that X was there—higher expenditures, decentralization, fragmentation— and it is rather a question whether it was X or something else that was causal. On the other hand, one variant of this strategy that does happen to be fairly reliably available is a search for the causal chain connecting X to Y—what George and McKeown (1985) call "process tracing." This, however, tends to and should place one in the mode of physical causal reasoning, to which we now turn.

If the small-n design is weak in principle in the light of factual causal reasoning ("in principle" because specific applications of any design may be persuasive for local reasons), perhaps it should be considered more as an extended case study using the method of physical causal reasoning. That is well enough if the findings in the two or more units are essentially corroborative, as for example in Barley's study of radiology in two hospitals. It strengthens the sense of having unearthed a meaningful finding when the same operative reason and resulting behavior shine through in two or more contexts. If the results are not corroborative, however—if, for example, reason X was also present in a second unit but the proposed causal effects did not manifest themselves as clearly—the investigator is in trouble. Why was this difference in outcome observed? The second unit, in other words, simply muddies the causal waters apparently clarified in the first. But furthermore, the temptation in such cases is usually to try to explain such a difference by a third factor, some dimension of the context that was present, let us say, in the first unit but absent in the second. What this strategy does, however, is to throw the design directly back into the category of factual causal reasoning. The attempt is to reason by variables and counterfactuals, saying or implying that if the third factor had been present in the second unit as well, then so would the hypothesized relation between X and Y. The mixing of the two types of causal reasoning is fine if one can pull it off successfully, but remember, as we have just seen, that the number of units is generally too small to sustain that kind of reasoning with validity in small-n research. It may easily be too difficult to say with confidence that it was indeed this particular third factor that made the difference, just as it was too difficult to pin causality to X itself under factual causal reasoning, as elaborated above. Recognizing this fragility of inference when results are not corroborative, the researcher must often end by speculating.

One might suppose that the two types of causal reasoning could somehow be made to complement one another, so that although neither was adequate alone the two together would make a strong causal case. What we imagine now, for example, is a case study oriented toward physical causal reasoning in country A that is not quite convincing about the causal relation between X and Y, and a complementary study in country B where not X was known to prevail and we also found that not Y prevailed. Unfortunately, this kind of complementation does not hold in principle, and for that reason I suggest that one would have difficulty making it sound persuasive in practice. The point is that the particular deficiencies in one causal design cannot be repaired by the logic of the other. The only causal information the second yields is information that we do not need and cannot use. If there is not enough information about the details of the physical causal relations in country A to make a good case that X (fragmentation) was the cause of Y (stability), then data on not X and not Y from country B cannot supply the missing physical detail: those data can only yield an additional type of causal inference that usually is also weak. Similarly, if we look at this design as one emphasizing factual causality—Y followed X in country A, and not Y followed not X in country B—and if the conclusion were challenged on the ground that the true causes of Y in country A may not have been X but instead some factors K that were absent in country B, then supplying a great deal of detail about physical causal relations in country A cannot mend the flaw. This physical causal reasoning in country A alone might very well add up to a good case for X and against K by the modus operandi method, but the fact that not X was accompanied by not Y in country B thereby becomes an extraneous bit of information, just as knowing that some accident victim B did not have either a heart attack (X) *or* a concussion (K) and managed to survive the crash does not help us decide whether victim A, who had both, died because of the concussion or the heart attack. Therefore, unless the additional units are corroborative or one is able simply to accept the comparability of subjects and contexts on relevant dimensions without needing to lean on a large sample for that purpose—which can indeed happen in some studies—we must apparently conclude that any small-n study is likely to be valuable in a causal sense only in suggesting hypotheses for future research. The sole basis on which some might conclude otherwise would seem to be the Bayesian sort of proposition that two weak studies are better than one, and I leave it to the Bayesians to decide whether the updating of priors on the basis of weak designs is a reasonable methodological practice or not.

It would be a mistake, however, to leave the analysis on that discouraging note. The mistake lies in looking primarily to factual causal reasoning for the gain when adding additional units of case study. It is only natural to do so because adding another city or district or country means "increasing the n," which should in turn mean mitigating the traditional weaknesses of the case study by moving the research closer to the surefootedness of the quantitative design. Supposedly, if we find not X and not Y in the second study, then the paradigm of factual causal reasoning suggests that we are in precisely the situation to which one aspires in large sample research except that we have few cases. If we find that X is present in the second unit but not Y, then we look for an additional factor K whose variation across the units of study will purportedly explain the observed difference in the causal efficacy of X. As we have seen, however, the standard factual causal reasoning in both types of instances is in principle unavailing in small-n research.

In light of the analysis of the previous sections, I suggest that better advantage of this research approach might be taken by sticking to physical causal reasoning rather than switching to factual causal reasoning as soon as the sample size is increased. The point is to use *multiple* case studies for clues to filling out the physical scenario connecting cause and effect in any *one* of them. Recall the importance I placed on understanding the process as a goal of research. I reviewed that notion as a method of attaining external validity, a basis for creative-selective generalization. It is clear, however, that understanding the process is also highly relevant to internal validity since explanation by physical causal reasoning will often mean showing that, in the real world, the process played itself out precisely as we would have expected it to if X were indeed the cause of Y (cf. subobjectives as design in Mohr 1995: 185–92). When this validation of the modus operandi occurs, it is difficult to doubt the causal role of X.

To elaborate, case studies of human social behavior do not focus on cause-and-effect relations as simple as billiard balls on the table or the nursing of one's toe. The forces and motions are subtle and contextual, often involving factors that help us grasp the motivations of individuals and groups to act as they did. If in the second unit studied we observe not X and not Y, for example, then the next step is to ponder the social mechanism that helps us to understand just how it was that X led to Y in the first unit, so that the absence of X understandably meant that Y would not occur in the second. The multiple sites are used to their fullest advantage when exploited in a search for meaningful contrasts or variation but not for the purpose of applying factual causal reasoning. In trying to attain a completely satisfying understanding of the stability that followed the socialist revolution in country A, for example, we might get the sense from studying country B that political and bureaucratic corruption were important in leading to the coup. To show that corruption was high in country B and low in country A means next to nothing by itself in the quest to establish left-wing fragmentation as the cause of stability. What is now necessary is to show vividly by the continued exploitation of case study techniques how the left-wing coalition in country B provided the operative reasons for corruption and how corruption then physically facilitated or provided the operative reasons for the coup d'etat; conversely, how fragmentation in country A affected resistance or alternatives to corruption; and how the absence of corruption frustrated the potential for a coup.

The task would be similar if we found X but not Y in the second unit except that we would then be seeking interactive rather than intervening dimensions of the context—more a why than a how. In the case of police expenditures and crime rates, for example, there might well be several interacting dimensions operating in tandem—a difference between the two cities in police corruption or mafia influence, perhaps (so that expenditures were efficacious only where such corruption was low); a difference in the place of key crime fighting units in the police power structure itself; or a difference in the level of education, qualifications, and skill of the police force. Again, documenting such differences alone means little because of the weakness of factual causal inference in the small-n context. The point is, rather, once a difference such as the contrasting internal power of key crime fighting units has been recognized, to show as vividly as possible how the power structure within the department led almost inexorably to allocating most of the additional resources to crime control in city A and to administrative overhead in city B. In the end, a convincing case is made for the causal relations in each of the two cities without really needing the contrasting results from the other. The contrast has served its function primarily in generating the ideas that could be pursued to fill out the physical causal explanation satisfactorily in each case.

In this way, maintaining a focus on physical causal reasoning—not allowing oneself to be distracted and diverted into factual causal thinking by the expansion of sample size to two or three—one can hope to achieve maximum internal validity within the small-n study. The design in this perspective is not really unique in type, for there are only two forms of causal reasoning, but is instead a variant of the case study. One ends indeed with several separate case studies, perhaps using some only to help in perfecting others, perhaps making a causal point about X and the parallel point about not X, perhaps emphasizing a certain dimension of the context, and perhaps making several quite different causal points. The advantage that this variant of the case study design confers lies in its potential for increasing the likelihood of completing a physical causal argument by the detailed empirical investigation of contrasting contexts under a similar conceptual regime. The primary function of the second and further cases is to reveal nuances of the first that might otherwise have been overlooked. In sum, from the standpoint of causality, the central purpose of comparison and contrast in small-n research should be to increase understanding and not to provide evidence for the counterfactual.

Let us apply these findings on small-n research to the constructive paper by Skocpol and Somers (1980) on a related topic, the uses of comparative history. Comparative history and comparative case studies are not exactly the same genre of research, but their reasoning is pertinent to our case as well. Analyzing a large number of important works in comparative history, the authors find three such uses: the parallel demonstration of theory, the contrast of contexts, and macrocausal analysis.

In the parallel demonstration of theory, multiple cases are treated to show that the unfolding of each is consistent with a particular explanatory theory. This is the sort of instance of small-n research in which the additional cases are supposedly corroborative, as in Barley's study of two hospitals. The proposed advantages lie first in the richness of detail provided by the variety of contexts and second in the confidence in the theory gained by its iterated support. The authors, however, do not accept the second advantage: "But no matter how many cases are discussed, the historical analyses themselves do not validate the theory. They can only illustrate and clarify it—and, potentially, refine it. This is because, quite obviously, the cases are selected in the first place in terms of the given theory. And the juxtaposed historical trajectories are not used to establish controls, only to show the theory at work again and again" (1980: 191). The language and argument indicate that the authors would rely primarily on contrast for theoretical validation—factual causal reasoning. On those grounds, their conclusion is obviously correct. There can be no demonstration of causality without evidence for the counterfactual. On the other hand, just one of the cases might potentially be enough to validate the theory (as it operated there) by physical causal reasoning. The additional cases would still not provide further validation, whatever that might mean, but core cause-and-effect relations would be established, the richness added could be consequential, and the repetition could add a sense of the importance or meaningfulness of the finding. The trouble with the approach even in that perspective is that many applications of it have involved a large number of cases, and not just two to four. In the some-what detailed description of eight or ten or twenty cases, space and energy are leeched away from the kind of deep description of one or two cases that would ordinarily be required to yield a persuasive phys-ical causal argument—the kind of probing of operative reasons and other physical forces that might lead to a true understanding of the process. Moreover, in the matter of external validity, if the research does not yield such an understanding of the modus operandi, no basis of generalizability is established no matter how many consistent cases are reviewed. Corroborative cases may indeed add richness, but the first duty in terms both of internal and external validity is to construct a strong physical causal argument, whether this requires one case or several.

As to the second use, the contrast of contexts, "much of the thrust of this variant of comparative history is to suggest that particular nations, empires, civilizations, or religions constitute relatively irre-ducible wholes, each a complex and unique sociohistorical configura-tion in its own right" (1980: 178). Thus, there is no attempt to use mul-tiple cases to support a common explanation of some frequent historical phenomenon. Rather, it is emphasized that similar forces will play themselves out differently, depending on context. Instead of seek-ing a causal explanation for Y, therefore, this approach for the most part seeks to elaborate the effects of X, which will differ with the cir-cumstances. It is close to the kind of case we have considered in which an additional unit of study manifests X but not Y. Skocpol and Somers see much good in the approach, especially in the rich, unfettered understanding of the individual cases, but they also note certain short-comings, again judging from the perspective of factual causal reason-ing: "Of course the price paid in Contrast-oriented comparative histo-ries is that descriptive holism precludes the development of explanatory arguments, even when these are implicitly present, crying to be drawn out of the comparative-historical materials. Independent and dependent variables are never explicitly distinguished, and the chronological account, 'telling the story,' is allowed to suffice as the mode of conveying understanding of what happened and why. . . . But the Contrast-oriented approach can also be theoretically very mislead-ing. For virtually any themes can be brought to bear upon the case materials without being put to any explicit test and without being openly identified as a proto-theory" (1980: 193). Thus, the central liability is bound up with the sense that *variables* are not specified so that they might be recognizable across cases and there is no testing, no striving toward historical generalization, and no explanatory argument developed out of the juxtaposition. What we have had in this approach in fact, and it is not necessarily a liability, is a *group* of case studies, each attempting to convey an understanding of historical events by a nearly self-conscious reliance on physical causal reasoning—certainly, at any rate, with a studious avoidance of reliance on the alternative. If we do not critique from the perspective of factual causal reasoning, then each case stands on its own, and validity depends on the quality of the physical causal argument in each. Care must be exercised in forging the collectivity: whatever holds such a collection of cases together and gives them a sense of unity of issue must do so without suggesting any hypothesis potentially supported by the set. The authors feel that historical theories do tend in fact to be latent in most applications of the approach, violating its first principles, and their account is persuasive on this point.

Last, we come to macro-causal analysis, where the terrain is completely familiar to practitioners of the counterfactual approach:

> a third group of scholars in fact uses comparative history primarily for the purpose of making causal inferences about macro-level structures and processes. . . . The logic involved in the use of comparative history for Macro-causal analysis resembles that of statistical analysis, which manipulates groups of cases to control sources of variation in order to make causal inferences. . . . The problem is that perfectly controlled comparisons are never really feasible. Societies cannot be broken apart at will into analytically manipulable variables, and history rarely, if ever, provides exactly the cases needed for controlled comparisons. . . . Moreover, even when the conclusions of a Macro-analytic comparative study do seem perfectly sound, there are still unavoidable difficulties about how to generalize the explanation beyond the historical cases actually included in the given study. . . . Unlike Contrast-oriented comparative history, it is arguable that Macro-analytic comparative history is better done in article format rather than in books. For it may be easier in articles to highlight causal arguments, to move freely back and forth across times and places, and to avoid the

temptations of presenting lengthy descriptive chronologies for their own sake. (1990: 181–82, 193–95)

Despite the problems cited, the authors encourage such studies. The results can be suggestive even if not definitive. Existing hypotheses can be tested and sometimes rejected with confidence, even if they rarely can be supported with confidence. The approach encourages the development of promising, alternative hypotheses about macrosocial phenomena. Although I am in substantial agreement with most of the authors' analysis and critique—excepting the somewhat lame bases for encouraging the approach in spite of its limitations—my own analysis clearly comes out quite differently. Unless the problems of chance and spurious relations happen not to be very severe in a given piece of research, the conclusion we reached earlier in this section is that this sort of reliance on factual causal reasoning in small-n research should be abandoned or should at least be supplemented by the approach via physical causation. The focus and aspiration of multiple units should be a thorough explication of the causal mechanism or modus operandi involved in any one or more of them, so that internal validity is attained with a high degree of confidence and no lame justifications are necessary.

In the Skocpol and Somers paper, then, we have a critique that greatly enriches our appreciation of small-n analysis by showing that it can be multifaceted in approach and varied in its goals. It has been my suggestion that even more of the potential may be realized when the approach is viewed without the confining constraint of a single conception of causality. The potential of small-n studies is substantial if the genre is turned loose epistemologically, that is, if it is not bound tightly to the causal paradigm that underlies large-n research.

Chapter 5

Explanation, Laws, and Theory

Our focus has been the causal explanation of behavior. It is true that a great deal of scholarship in the social disciplines does not have causal explanation as a goal or orientation. But a great deal of it does, in all of the disciplines, and even when an explanation of why people do things or did things is not the direct purpose of the inquiry, still, as long as the subject is somehow the behavior of people, no matter how indirectly, basic ideas about how behavior comes about are likely to be pertinent. In this chapter, we look more pointedly at the nature of the explanations we may develop within the framework elaborated in the preceding chapters.

Causal Explanation and Causal Laws

A central aim of this study is to endorse and be able to explain the following paradox: concerning human behavior, there is always a social science explanation that is causal and "lawful" (i.e., that shows the phenomena as being covered by laws or as instantiating one or more laws), but there are no causal laws governing human behavior. The latter assertion is based on the hypothesis that the production of any such behavior depends categorically on encounters, and, there being no physical causes of encounters, no events that depend on encounters can be governed by physical laws. In other words, the paradox is an instance of a more general principle: there is always an explanation of a physical encounter that is causal and lawful, but there are no causal laws governing encounters.

Clearly, the validity of the statement depends on the difference between causal explanations and causal laws. How, first, is the explanation of an encounter causal and lawful? It is so in the sense that *once we know* that a certain encounter has taken place at time $t + 1$, which means we know that precisely those causes and conditions needed to produce the encounter were in place as required at time *t*, we can explain the encounter causally with a base at time *t* by showing the physical causes of the changes in each of the two (or more) constituent elements of the encounter (e.g., two cars or billiard balls) between the earlier time and the later. For example, suppose that two billiard balls have collided on the table. Then, given the initial position, matter, and motion of each of the balls, and given as well the other circumstances or aspects of the physical causal scenario that prevailed, the encounter between them was completely determined by and is explained by physical laws. In a clear, direct, nongimmicky sense, the explanation is deterministic, causal, and lawful. Note, however, that both the qualifier "in the circumstances" and the known occurrence of the encounter are critical givens of the explanation. Without these, no laws would determine the outcome. In particular, causal chains containing preliminary encounters are at issue here; that is, causal chains that amount essentially to the process by which each ball or each car arrived at the collision point. In this light, the reference to "the physical causal scenario" or the stipulation "in the circumstances" is essentially a guarantee that things would turn out the way they did. That is, because the circumstances of the universe were precisely as they were, any preliminary encounters that may have been necessary for the balls or cars to arrive at the required place-time, such as an encounter with a certain curvature of the table or with a green rather than a red light, were indeed bound to occur. Moreover, because the collision between the balls or cars actually did occur, it is clear that the circumstances were such that no interfering encounters from any source were on track to prevent the ultimate collision.

Why then do we say that no causal laws govern the encounter? This is true because no laws concerning a specified set of objects or other phenomena (together with initial conditions) can entail any real-world encounter that has not yet taken place. In each instance of the action of the law, its fulfillment must depend on a new variety of chance occurrences. For example, no laws applied to two billiard balls and a specified set of circumstances entail that the balls will collide, even if we try to take full account of their initial positions. In the circumstances, in fact—and here we refer to the unspecified circumstances—they may very well not collide because of a tiny blemish in the table top that we didn't know about, a fatal weakness in one of the table legs, an impending earthquake, the self-destruction of one of the balls at the last moment, and so on. No set of conditions can be stipulated that entails the collision of two billiard balls either in general or in any one specific instance.

I take the following to be the critical difference between the two clauses of the paradox: an explanation of an encounter can be causal and lawful because it can be completely post hoc and can refer *globally and nonspecifically* to the precise circumstances that did in fact obtain; that is, it can refer without naming. Thus, because we know that an encounter has occurred, we no longer have to worry about unspecified circumstances that might have prevented it, and we can see each of the two contributing streams of events, in the absence of interference of any sort, as having followed the pure laws of nature. We are then able to name certain initial conditions, such as initial position and motion, and show that in the (precise but unspecified) circumstances, the laws of force and motion entail that the two were bound to collide and in a certain way—in fact, in exactly the way they did. A causal law itself, however, must specify both what would (and not just what did) happen to Y under various values of X as well as the circumstances under which the stated relation obtains. Such covering laws will specify how any balls will proceed if nothing interferes and no initial assumptions about them are wrong, but they cannot take specific account of everything that might ever be amiss in these two ways. In general, the Newtonian physical laws of motion stipulate the momentum that will be transferred to any body by a specific force once the force has been applied to that body. In this the laws are presumably always correct, and beyond this they do not venture. In particular, they can in themselves determine neither that a force *will be* applied to a given body nor what the body will do after the application—for example, how far it will travel and what it might bump into. (A force that is continuously applied, such as gravity, always has its effect, but the effect does not go beyond the imparting of momentum. It does not specify the subsequent empirical behavior of the body to which it is applied, which depends on other objects, forces, and circumstances.)

Let us return now to intentional behavior. The production of behavior involves a great many physiological encounters, but as social scientists we are interested primarily in just a few of them. The causal chain may be quite long, but the critical links for us are those that occur within the affect-object system. Knowing the approximate rudiments of the system, we know that we can refer to these links as desires, decisions, goals, and particularly reasons. Reasons not only explain behavior in a rational framework; they are factual causes in the sense of occupying a necessary physical slot in a causal chain that produces the behavior. This means that once the occurrence of the behavior has been stipulated and the actual circumstances are taken as given (so that the position of "strongest" and the two satellite decisions are all guaranteed), the reason is a good, sound, law-covered, causal explanation for the behavior.

Although reasons are causes in this sense, there can be no generalized law of the sort that says that whenever a person has a reason to do something he or she will do it. Nor can there be a more specific law saying that whenever a person has reason R to perform behavior B he or she will do that. The laws that are pertinent to the production of intentional behavior are the same as those that are pertinent to billiard balls—Newton's laws and the edifice that physics and chemistry have built upon them. Reasons as they occur in the affect-object system are physical, but just as the laws cannot determine that one billiard ball will collide with another and cause it to move away in a certain manner, they also cannot determine that a reason will cause a behavior. Encounters necessarily intervene; that is, there is room for all sorts of interference between times t and $t + 1$—for example, between the onset of the reason and the performance of the behavior. In the case of behavior, one critical encounter is the encounter of a reason with other reasons. Whether a senator who wants to improve his or her attendance record will hurry to the chamber to vote depends on *what else* the senator wants at the time and on which desire is physiologically strongest. The latter depends in turn on the association of objects with other objects, on the affect attached to each, and on which objects and associations are activated. All of these depend on further encounters, most of them having taken place in the individual's past life. Furthermore, no amount of specification of circumstances can make such a cause of behavior lawlike unless the specification of circumstances be complete, that is, unless it refers to every element that might possibly interfere in instances covered by the law. The message is therefore clear: there are no laws or systematic generalizations that will accurately characterize human behavior, and there is no point in chasing them. Our conclusion here is a bit different from most former statements of this nature, however, in that it is accompanied by the allied principles that (*a*) social science does not differ in this respect from physical science—there are no laws or applications of laws governing encounters in which physical scientists might have an interest—and (b) in spite of there being no laws, intentional human behavior is physically caused, and operative reasons are the physical causes.

In this light, social science has differed from physical science in two ways, one a matter of practice and the other a matter of principle. The first is that in practice physical scientists have rarely attempted to discover laws governing the sorts of behavior that depend on encounters. They have not, for example, tried to generate deterministic laws governing the weather, the height of mountains, or the life span of stars (with forecasting models of such things as the weather being definitely seen as correlational forecasting models and not as causal laws). In contrast, this is precisely what we have tried to do in social science when we have sought generalizations, for example, that innovation is caused by status and effectiveness motives, that history is cyclical, that participation in decision making causes greater productivity, and so on. In neither physical nor social science can any of these be laws. There is in fact only one set of basic laws of nature, and it has been the mistake of some to think that each discipline might have its own—governing its own encounters of interest.

The second way in which the two differ is that encounters tend to be far more regular, predictable, and manageable in much of the matter studied in physical science than they are in social science. In the former, predictions that involve encounters can often be successfully made under the specification of a few key circumstances, and ideas involving encounters can be tested fairly reliably. For example, the trajectory of a rocket or a bullet depends heavily on encounters, but not much is likely to interfere (especially with the latter). Given data on certain conditions, one's calculations can be relied upon with substantial confidence. In comparison, it is folly to think in most significant cases that a given reason is quite certain not to be outweighed by any other possible reasons. We may observe an empirical relation connecting a reason and an action, but it will not in general be very regular even in one population and time period and is quite likely to be substantially different when replication is attempted within dissimilar populations.

There is a tendency to see many events in the physical and biological worlds as being physically caused when technically these events are either encounters or are dependent upon encounters. There are two reasons for this, I believe, one being that the actual instances of physical causation in the chain are quite obvious and create the dominant impression of overall physical causation and the other that the outcome is highly probable, often approaching a probability of 1 even though encounters are involved. Consider, for example, the old carnival concession at which people who wanted to demonstrate their strength would try to ring a bell by swinging a heavy mallet, striking the end of a large lever, and sending a metal clapper straight up a track toward a bell at the top. If they rang the bell, they won a cigar. Suppose that Clancy rang the bell. There would be a tendency to think that the blow of the mallet was the physical cause of the ringing of the bell, even though encounters necessarily intervened. The mechanics are both clear and physical, and the outcome is almost certain provided the game is fair.

This reasoning shows the meaning of a "machine." A machine is a device, whether natural or artificial, that makes certain encounters so highly probable as virtually to guarantee the occurrence of a particular event that depends on them. If you put the chunks of meat and other materials in one end of a sausage-making machine and press the button, out of the other end will come a proper sausage—nearly 100 percent of the time. The same predictability holds for an automobile as well, although such is the intricacy of this particular type of machine that the probability of reliable functioning is perhaps not quite so high. A similar predictability is found in virtually all important biological processes as well, such as the construction of proteins and the overcoming of minor infections. These processes are full of encounters (a major point in the well-known work by Monod [1971])—the actual bumping of molecules and cells in fact—but evolution has so fashioned the machine that the encounters are virtually assured.

I want to urge, however, that Clancy's receipt of the cigar—not only the ringing of the bell—is the outcome of just such a machine and should be seen as such, in spite of the fact that the instances of physical causation in the chain are not so obvious nor so clearly physical. There are rules of the game stating that Clancy is to be awarded a cigar by the concessionaire, and there are social norms forcing upon the concessionaire the necessity of abiding by those rules. These rules and norms play upon reasons (motives). The actual award, as a result, is as highly probable as the output of many a more obvious machine, and the instances of physical causation in the chain are in truth no less physical. This is a social machine, and we have a great many of them—various sets of rules and norms, institutions such as marriage and elections, and so on. Neither the production of the sausage, the conquest of the infection, nor the incumbency of the victor are effects of simple physical causation; all are rather outcomes of causal chains in which machines have arranged for the occurrence of the necessary encounters. The social machines are all the more impressive creations in that the important encounters they virtually assure are in general less manageable in nature than those in most of the more clearly physical machines.

I have, then, indicated two ways in which physical and social science have differed, with the problem for social science being that encounters, which defy systematic generalization, make up almost all of its subject matter. However, a fundamental similarity is observed to shine through these differences. The two sets of disciplines are similar in that both are concerned with and are able to provide law-covered causal explanations of encounters and of events that depend on them. Whenever we in social science make a persuasive case that certain operative reasons were responsible for a particular behavior, for example, that the U.S.-Soviet arms race was powered in large measure by the needs of the respective economies, we are doing exactly what a geologist would be doing in making the case that a meteor that landed somewhere in the Caribbean was the cause of the great Cretaceous die-off. When we explain a behavior with reasons, in other words, we are not using the rational paradigm alone. We are also saying that the behavior did occur and, given the reasons and the particular circumstances that obtained in actuality, the laws of Newton, Faraday, and so on, determined the outcome.

The Myth of Probabilistic Laws

It is sometimes claimed that there are indeed laws in our disciplines, but probabilistic ones. This is meant to allow some leeway in the specification of the conditions under which a law is operative, such that if the law does not, because it cannot, specify all of the pertinent qualifying conditions, it might contain most of them, or at least the important ones. Predictions would then have a margin of error, but the laws would be basically sound. Unfortunately, those who suggest that social science has probabilistic laws rarely suggest, even roughly, what sort of *content* such laws might have. We must then use our own judgment in speculating on the possibilities.

To begin pursuit of the inquiry, let us accept the semantic ground rule that there is something categorically unlawlike about the statement "X sometimes causes Y." Such a relation might well be probabilistic, but let us agree that in this vague form it is not a *law*, otherwise we would have to allow almost any causal relation to be in itself a law. In this perspective, we will see that there can be no probabilistic laws of human behavior because there is nothing constraining probabilistic explanations of human behavior to be stable.

If there were to be a probabilistic law of human behavior, what sort of content would it have? Suppose that a study has shown a strong causal impact of the size of organizations upon their innovativeness. If 70 percent of the large organizations in a given population were innovative, for example, one might suggest the probabilistic law that large organizations have a .7 probability of being innovative. Few would make such a claim, however, given the high likelihood that other populations of large organizations would show 65, 71, 30, or 99 percent innovativeness, so that the "law" might just as easily stipulate "a .65 probability," and so on. If one measured all past and present large organizations and found that 70 percent fell into the "innovative" category, that figure would still not represent a law but rather a simple population proportion, with the population having a time boundary at today's date (Scriven 1959: 464). If this were a law, then all such population proportions would be laws, and the laws would change as time progressed and altered the proportions. In concept, something more appears to be necessary for a relation to count as a law—some quality of "natural necessity" (Beauchamp 1974)—and that quality is generally missing in social science. The fact is that whether a large organization will be innovative does not depend on a natural necessity that links size and innovation but on probabilistic encounters, and the encounters governing human behavior—in particular the encounter of reasons with other reasons—are inherently unlawlike. The histories and contextual arrangements of large organizations are not intrinsically such as to make 70 percent of them innovative.

Furthermore, few social scientists would suggest a probabilistic law with the sort of content we have been considering because it says nothing about small organizations. If 70 percent of the small organizations were innovative as well, there would clearly be no pretense to a law connecting size and innovation. Perhaps the content, then, must derive from a regression coefficient or something comparable. If the causal impact of size upon innovation in a study were a powerful 1.3 (to take some arbitrarily scaled magnitude), we might be tempted to generalize that figure to a probabilistic law. But the figure 1.3 taken alone represents a deterministic claim, not a probabilistic one, so that we must add to the law the information that there is a normally distributed random error with a variance of, say, 5.08. This means that, given any score on organization size, each possible innovation score has a distinct probability of occurrence. Note that the error variance that is stipulated—the probabilistic part of the claim—cannot be just "something," or we would have violated our initial ground rule. It must somehow be specified as part of the law. By the same reasoning employed above based on encounters, however, any specific error variance would still be devoid of intrinsic necessity, and that defect would no doubt be reflected in the instability both of the coefficient and the error variance across studies.

To expand on this, is it not the probabilistic character of encounters, rather than natural necessity, that conduces to probabilistic laws? The answer is "only if that probabilistic character is stable." According to at least some scholars (e.g., Suppes 1984), there are probabilistic laws describing phenomena in physics—laws governing the parameters of radioactive decay, for example. These laws, however, are grounded in a describable natural process featuring a particular sort of probabilistic foundation: each is supposed to represent a strictly random process under constant contextual conditions—for example, a crowd of wildly bouncing particles escaping from a sheath from time to time through tiny pores. Similarly, Mendel's laws of segregation and independent assortment essentially stipulate the strictly random distribution of alleles to gametes, making possible the further probabilistic laws of phenotypic outcome in sexual reproduction. Under the stipulated or presumed conditions, it is the fact of these strictly random processes at work in the encounters that give the laws their probabilistic rather than deterministic character. Further (and somewhat paradoxically), it is the utter stability of any genuinely random process that gives these probabilistic events the character of a law. Randomness produces highly reliable results. To be comparable, innovation would have to be a strictly random process (thus not categorizable as intentional behavior at all!), and organizational size would have to be taken under constant contextual conditions. The effects of the operative reasons that govern human behaviors are not, however, random. Under constant conditions, they should produce deterministic and not probabilistic laws.

In our case, probabilistic character derives rather from the variability of conditions in the "scenario" or "circumstances," each context bringing an individualized collection of additional reasons, memories, and sensory impressions into the affect-object field, and featuring also the behavior of other people and objects, and each being thereby capable of influencing behavioral outcomes in its own way. Does this yield a probabilistic law? Only, we must concede, if the resulting error distribution is stable. One might specify a given set of determining conditions and hope that variation in other relevant conditions will always produce the same distribution of error, but that hope is vain in principle because these other encounters are not random. They are also determined, varying according to definite dimensions of culture and cultural change, environment, competition, wars, recessions, local behaviors, and other major and minor forces. If by reinforcing and offsetting one another they were discovered frequently to produce the same net effect on innovation, it would be happenstance. There is no basis for expecting such a result to be faithfully reproduced. We may like to think of the excluded causal forces as a "stochastic" component operating across the subjects in any one piece of research, but when we begin to think about "laws" we quickly realize that the content of this component is not, in actuality, random. The juxtaposition of excluded variables with each other and with the included ones is indeed a set of encounters. There is no basis except "assumption" for expecting the excluded causes to be random with respect to the included ones in a second population or time period, even if they were in a first population and time period, and there is no basis even so for expecting them to be present in the same magnitudes in the second study. On the contrary, the error distribution (and therefore the explained variance) must be expected in principle to fluctuate inexplicably.

Thus, whether there is a sound basis for probabilistic laws in areas of physics and biology or not, there are no such laws governing human behavior. That is true, in summary, because neither the causation specified in a theory nor the unnamed causal forces summarized in its error term may by any stretch be considered to be random processes. Thus, there is no basis for an expectation that they will be jointly stable, and, indeed, they have never been found to be so. Unlike the cases of radioactive decay and the production of gametes, we are therefore confronted with instability in the level of probability at which an event or causal relation will occur. It turns out that we can do little more than to say that "X sometimes causes Y." The relations are indeed probabilistic, but they are not laws.

Humbled by the requirements of concreteness for a respectable probabilistic law, we might venture the very modest but still definite formulation that the relation between size and innovation is always positive (Lijphart 1971: 686). This fails to be a law again, however, and for precisely the same reasons as before. There is nothing that constrains the relationship in populations to be positive. The result is basically an accident of research design. We realize full well that there are a great many large but *non*innovative organizations in the world as well as numerous small but innovative ones. The "law" would rest ultimately on the hope that we never happened to observe a particular group of organizations in which these perverse types were in the majority, making the relation between size and innovation negative. Even if the hope were fulfilled in our experience, this would not change the accidental character of the finding.

Finally, by a probabilistic law one might mean simply that the relation in question is always strong or the causal impact always substantial, but with some error. By the same reasoning, again, there is no law here: if "strong" is defined as "greater than .8," for example, we are merely hoping against a .79.

There is in this last formulation, however, something genuinely noteworthy. We have in such an observation of compelling strength, presumably based on several studies, not a law but a stimulus to further research; not an end but a beginning. Why has this connection been observed? Is it trivial (the higher the heat and humidity, the more crowded the beaches; the weaker the economy relative to the rest of the world, the lower the immigration pressure), or does it provide valuable insight? Consider the latter possibility. If, for example, we find a strong tendency for economic conditions to affect the electoral fortunes of the incumbent party or for oligarchic tendencies to arise once a threshold of organizational size and age has been exceeded, we may be led by the skill and powers of the researchers involved to achieve so solid an understanding of the phenomenon at issue that we are willing to recognize the findings as *theoretically* meaningful. It is enough, however, to find such consistently strong observations interesting and important and to investigate them further. There is no need to overlook their inherent instability—to use them to try to aggrandize social science or draw similar comfort by loosely and misleadingly seeking to elevate them to the status of probabilistic laws.

Moreover, an orientation toward probabilistic laws can be destructive. The notion that one has a law, or is working toward one, tends to confer a degree of satisfaction or reinforcement in and of itself, one that distracts attention from the uncomfortable question of just how interesting and important the relations at issue really are, lawlike or not. Social scientists have been known to feel that they are on to something valuable when they document the existence of almost any statistically significant relationship, but when we internalize the fact that there are no laws, not even probabilistic ones, the recording of a relationship has little more intrinsic interest than the recording of a single instance of alleged causation. In either case, and given that the issue can be considered important, it then becomes germane to ask the twin questions "Were the causal relations involved convincingly established?" and "Do we understand them well enough to be able to generalize them effectively?"

Explanation and Theory

We have noted that, whereas all intentional behavior is physically caused, social scientists commonly go about the business of the causal explanation of behavior either by physical or by factual causal reasoning. Another dichotomy appears to be similar to this one but is actually independent and speaks to aims rather than means. One might view the two aims of explanatory research as having been, in practice, the development of singular explanations for human action and the development of generalizations, especially systematic generalizations. I wish to explore these aims in light of the previous analysis and thereby to search out a sensible perspective on the roles of social research. In the process, I would like to collapse this dichotomy and so do away with it. That is, I want to try to obviate some of the major distinctions that are currently made between types of social science—between camps—such as general and singular, scientific and historical. With regard to the aim of producing valid generalizations, I have of course argued that the development of laws of behavior in social science is not possible. This does not mean that there is no point to research carried out for the sake of generalization, but it does mean that we must confront the issue of how such research is to be viewed given that this ultimate aim is categorically frustrated. Let us turn first, however, to singular explanation.

By singular explanation I mean explanation that does not pretend to be valid for a specified class of events but only for one member of such a class or perhaps a limited number of members. One might explain, for example, why Napoleon invaded Russia, or why American business lost ground to the Japanese in the 1970s, or why the suicide rate is so high among women of the Gainj in Papua New Guinea (Johnson 1981). Such explanation is found commonly in the disciplines of history and anthropology, but it permeates all of the other social disciplines as well.

An important and fundamental question is why, in academic social research, we should be interested in providing singular explanations. A singular explanation always explains the past. What good can that do? *Why study history?* It is clear that human beings are addicted to stories, that is, to accounts of the causes and consequences of human action, and perhaps as individuals one can say that these accounts and stories help us to regulate our own affairs. But the question might well be raised whether that is enough to justify the activity of large segments of several major academic disciplines. It is difficult to say precisely why we are so committed to learning about the way in which certain things happened in the past, but I do not foresee the slightest diminution in the inclination to remain so committed. Somehow, we do feel—and I simply accept this as a valid orientation—that an understanding of important past events is valuable, even when we recognize that such understanding cannot be extended *in any systematic way* to the prediction, explanation, or control of future events (Scriven 1966: 250).

This provides us with a clue in our quest for a perspective on the roles of social research: good research and ideas are apparently those that impart this sort of understanding of the past, with the proviso that such understanding must be useful.

In terms of the major components of research design, understanding relates primarily to internal validity. The idea is to impart through the research a consummate causal understanding of the past behavior under investigation, such that all pertinent challenges and questions regarding that past behavior and our explanation of it are answerable from the data and their logical extensions. Thus, the lesson of the value of the study of the past when we cannot make the homogeneity assumption is that we are subject to a more exacting criterion of internal validity than that of coming as close as possible to establishing that a connection is causal. When the effect to be explained is a human behavior in some form, *external* validity requirements will generally impose the extra burden of coming as close as possible to producing a consummate understanding of the relation, and this will be affected primarily by the set of events or variables we choose to investigate and the quality of the measurements, analyses, and presentation. Understanding as a goal of research is a venerable idea. The well-known *verstehen* approach has an institutionalized position in the philosophy of social science that is often seen as a rebuttal and alternative to positivism (a brief summary pertinent to the present discussion may be found in Warnke [1984]; see also Scriven [1966], 250–54). What is different in the present treatment, without attempting a philosophical exposition, is that understanding here *embraces* the notion of causation rather than setting itself up in opposition to it.

Establishing a causal connection between organizational size and innovation, for example, may be a reasonable start toward understanding that relation, but as it stands the nature of the connection is encased in a black box, and generalization will therefore be difficult. Recall that generalization must inevitably be selective and creative. The idea is that particular research on size and innovation should be instructive in thinking about the same or a similar issue in new contexts. Perhaps in the very next few time periods, the same relation may reasonably be expected to hold in the same populations of organizations, but as we change populations, or leave the time period far behind, then whether we can apply these findings at all, and whether fully or partially, will depend on *relevant* similarities between the two contexts. Moreover, just which dimensions are relevant is in turn likely to be revealed only through an understanding of the modus operandi of size upon innovation. In social science, the particular research project or program of research does not induce nor even test a strict regularity. The present analysis supports the argument that what it does at best, and instead, is present us with a *significant possibility* (Scriven 1966: 246–51)—a way in which behavior frequently does indeed unfold, even if not always (possibility), and a finding that is important for the world to know about (significant).

Thus, the best explanatory research is research that generates strong causal insight into human affairs, where by the inclusive term "strong causal insight" I mean the three concepts just referred to: research that imparts (*a*) a "consummate causal understanding" of a relation such that we are presented with (*b*) a "significant possibility" that we can use by means of (*c*) "creative-selective generalization" to illuminate and inform possible iterations of this relation in other contexts. In this sense, it is wrong to denigrate a strong causal insight such as the theory of cognitive dissonance (Festinger 1962), for example, or the theory that morale affects productivity (Roethlisberger and Dickson 1939), on the grounds that it does not hold in all cases. The danger may lie more in our ever thinking that it might. If a theory does indeed present a significant possibility, it stands at a high level of accomplishment within social science and indeed at the highest level possible within the area of explanatory theory.

We may now note explicitly what has begun to become clear, namely, that any quantitative findings short of universal laws are very much in the same category as singular explanations. They do not target a single event, it is true, but whichever individuals and events (such as adopting innovations, going to war, and so on) they do target must nevertheless be seen as singular in an important respect: they cannot stand for or refer accurately to a class of similar events covered by a universal law. A quantitative finding about the determinants of political participation, class mobility, or the persuasiveness of communications is a singular explanation in that, in the strict sense, it applies only to the population, context, and time period sampled, even when modified and updated by later studies in the best tradition of cumulative research. Inherently, it is impossible to know just when the quantitative findings arising from such studies will apply outside of the original and now past context of the research. For that reason, surprisingly enough, statistical research becomes "historical" research (Gergen 1973), and it again becomes difficult to say in concrete terms why one would want to pursue such inquiry, particularly when the predictive power and accuracy of the limited generalizations we do develop have in practice been so meager. Apparently, the answer here must be the same as in the more obvious varieties of singular explanation: we are interested in the creative-selective generalization of significant possibilities.

Quantitative research can indisputably arrive at generalizations if what is meant by that is generalizing to a population rigorously sampled. However, the explanation of behavior offered in such research would still be a singular explanation in that the population and time period implicated would still represent only a limited case. This is not a picky point. We know from a persuasive amount of experience that the explanations shift significantly as the population shifts, new populations are studied, or certain dimensions of the environment change with the passage of time (see, for example, Mohr 1982: 7–34). True, the results of such research may easily be valid as well for a great many cases outside of the population actually studied or sampled, but the same may be said for nonquantitative research. Michels' (1959) iron law of oligarchy, which was generated from a few case studies implemented without benefit of the methodology of objectivity, is one clear example. Its lesson is not universally valid (Lipset et al. 1956), but it is apparently true in most cases that the governance of an organization will tend toward oligarchy even when the organization promotes democratic values as its major output (certain labor unions, political parties, etc.). In both approaches, then, (*a*) the insight may be valid for large numbers of individuals or groups, past, present, and future, and (*b*) the mapping of that validity is impossible. The dimensions of generalizability are indeterminate no matter how many conditions or circumstances are specified as part of the "law." Quantitative research is necessary when it is important to explain behavior in a group or population, when the frequency of occurrence and not just the possible existence of a relation is important to us, or when the subject matter is such that quantitative rather than qualitative methods are most likely to yield strong causal insight. Electoral behavior, for example, may in general be such an area (not meaning to imply, of course, that all quantitative research in electoral behavior will yield strong insights). It was at least a moderately strong causal insight to discover in the 1950s that identification with a political party, presumably as a result of childhood socialization, was a powerful determinant of the vote of individuals (Campbell et al. 1960). The insight arose out of data on national samples of the United States, and it is doubtful that it could possibly have achieved the status of an insight had only a few intensive case studies of individuals been conducted. It happens that the importance of party identification in the American electorate has waxed and waned since the 1950s, but the value of the insight is not diminished. What we truly learned is that affective identification with parties or other symbols must in general be given careful consideration when searching for explanations for political choice. In just the same way, the value of the iron law of oligarchy as a strong causal insight is not diminished by the discovery of one or more counterexamples.

Thus, the answer to the question of the importance of the numbers of individuals studied is that everything depends on the quality of the individual application of the method and not on the method itself. One can have absolutely no confidence that one is doing the right or best thing in social science by using either large sample research or a case study. Case studies of highly momentous events, as well as correlations applying to the American electorate, British industrial firms, all recorded wars, and the like, even if the relations involved are shown to have been causal, do not necessarily produce good social theory. Good theory depends on such things as how important the explanations are and how widely and effectively we feel we may be able to use those explanations in the process of creative-selective generalization, given that we cannot use them universally. How widely and well we can use them, in turn, depends on how creatively reality has been conceptualized, how persuasively concepts have been captured by measurements, and how deep and thorough an understanding of the process is conveyed by the explanation. It seems to me that most methods in use in social science—formal modeling, case studies, large-sample research, and so on—have shown themselves susceptible to being used both well and poorly, that is, they are capable of supporting good theoretical ideas as well as of being rather a waste of time.

Kuhn (1962) referred to what he called "normal science." This is research on a certain topic that follows in the wake of the seminal scholarship on that topic. It is often considered that the function of normal science is to amplify, specify, or otherwise elaborate or modify the basic laws originally propounded in the seminal research. Perhaps it works that way in those sciences that do deal in the discovery of universal or nearly universal laws about the working of the natural world, but it follows from the foregoing that we must be a little careful about normal science in the social disciplines. Because there are no laws (beyond the physical ones), laws cannot be elaborated. Normal science must apparently relate to seminal scholarship—elaborating and modifying it, perhaps, or discovering some of the conditions under which it has been valid or has failed to be valid—but should not hope to provide the conditions that will make the original insight into a law by explaining away a piece of the original error variance. The latter orientation has, I think, been a distraction. By thinking about what normal science can properly hope to do in social science, I believe it will become clear that it should function in large measure to provide more modest insights that supplement and fill out the original, strong insights. It appears to me that this orientation has been lacking and that a rethinking of normal science in the social disciplines might on that basis increase its value. This set of ideas about seminal theory and normal science has been framed by a senior scholar in social psychology (Smith 1976) as follows:

> It is odd that "laws" figure so prominently in the present debate, when social psychologists as a tribe are so little impressed by the workmanlike propositional inventory assembled by Berelson and Steiner (1964). What many of us are likely to think of first are "landmark" studies or research programs, which seem to me typically to have the character of *demonstrations* identifying, legitimizing, and publicizing a new way of looking at some aspect of social phenomena.

> In this vein we take pride in such classics as M. Sherif on social norms via the autokinetic phenomenon (1936) and (with C. Sherif) on the evocation and reduction of intergroup conflict (1953); in Lewin, Lippitt and White (1939) on climates of leadership; in Asch on conformity (1951) and on forming impressions of personality (1946); in Hovland, Janis and Kelley (1953) on persuasive communication; in Schachter on affiliation (1959) and on cognition and emotion (1970). Each of these works opened new vistas, and each in turn launched a spate of research to elaborate upon the initial work or to correct it, to suggest alternative interpretations.

> We also admire the experimental launching of middle-range theories or explanatory models, such as those involving cognitive dissonance, balance, causal attribution, and exchange or equity. Again, the secure harvest lies in what Gergen (1973) referred to as sensitization. With such research behind us, we think of social phenomena in a less naive, more differentiated way than we did before. Sensitization is not to be sneezed at!

> Disenchantment begins to set in as attempts to go beyond demonstration and sensitization to parametric exploration and quantita-

tive formalization [are launched, but these] never seem to begin to provide secure components ready for Newtonian or even Darwinian synthesis.

Before closing with two broad issues concerning social theory and general laws, I would like to return momentarily to the question "Why study history?" The answer I suggested emphasized an inherently vague utility: there is a strong sense in which the study of the past is potentially useful in prosecuting the affairs of the future even if the application of such knowledge cannot be systematic, that is, even if we do not know precisely to which situations in the present and future the insights regarding the past may be applicable. Generalization may be powerful, but it is creative-selective at best. My discussion of the implications of this conclusion related primarily to what might be called theoretical research, with the aspiration toward laws being replaced by an aspiration toward the derivation of significant possibilities.

In this light, it is well to point out that the application to the future is not always quite so vague. Even though the precise circumstances to which the knowledge applies is uncertain, there may at least be certainty as to the kind of situation to which we *would like* the knowledge to apply, and indeed these applications may be the motivation for carrying out the research in the first place. I propose that we have here the distinction between theoretical and applied research: the latter is undertaken for the sake of an application that is known and certain at least in part and the former, conversely, for the vague utility that we have discussed in this section. Putting a major defining characteristic of theoretical research in this way, especially as a partial replacement for the goal of discovering general laws, brings theoretical research considerably closer in function to applied research than many, at least, have considered it to be in the past. With the methods being similar, as they always have been, and the goals now distinguished only by concreteness versus vagueness in intended application, the two are apparently not so very far apart. Note that as to applicability, even a program evaluation has its irreducible uncertainty. The conclusions are valid for the program of the past, as it was when it was studied, which is potentially different in unknown dimensions of context from the same program as it is now and will be tomorrow. In practice, the line between the two types of research will often be difficult to draw; that is, it will be questionable whether a given study belongs in one category or the other. In principle, this distinction is clear enough, and it is important as well in that it maintains a theoretical arena for social science. But it seems in this light not to be so great a distinction that it should divide social scientists into walled camps or divide their work invidiously into levels of value. The conceptual distance is too short; it is too easy to slip over from the one to the other.

Chapter 6

Rationality and Fitness: Two Broad Theories of Intentional Behavior

In the five previous chapters, I tried in part to show that universal, covering-law models of human behavior are not possible except insofar as the basic laws employed are the laws of physics—as expressed, let us say, in a mechanism such as the affect-object system. Even then, the laws do not "cover" behavior in the predictive sense because behavior depends on encounters, so that under any specified conditions, predictions will be accurate only when the needed encounters, whatever they are, do occur and the undesirable ones, whatever they are, do not. The physical laws pertinent to the generation of behavior can only determine the momentum transferred to individual molecules and other objects but cannot determine which such objects will be juxtaposed in what ways with which others and therefore what the specific behavioral outcomes will be. In this chapter, I would like to explore the question whether a universal, covering-law model might still be possible—without resort to physical mechanisms—by appeal either to rationality or to fitness as the basic explanatory principle.

Rationality and Universals

Considering rationality first, such a model would hold that the behavior of individuals is rationally determined, that is, that individuals have goals and beliefs and that they behave in such a way as to accomplish their goals efficiently given their beliefs. The model should in this view be a universal law on the assumption that human beings are, after all, inherently rational creatures: their intentional behavior should be found to be constrained systematically by the rational paradigm.

The possibility of such a covering-law model is suggested both in philosophy and in most social science disciplines. The primary mention in philosophy occurs in Hempel's (1963) reply to the critique by Dray (1957) of the covering-law model of human behavior, that is, of the philosophical position that the human and physical sciences are unified in method because behavior in both is covered by universal laws. Hempel objects to Dray's inclination to see behavior as being unlawlike because it follows a *rational* principle of action. He suggests that if people do indeed behave according to a rational principle, then their behavior is still lawlike. Both prediction and explanation must conform to a syllogism in which the third step cites a universal, empirical law, as follows:

> Agent A was in a situation of kind C.
> A was a rational agent at the time.
> Any rational agent, when in a situation of kind C, will invariably (or: with high probability) do X.
>
> Therefore, A did X. (Hempel 1963: 152–58)

Given our earlier discussion of the myth of probabilistic laws, we must decline to attach any significance in this context to the parenthetical expression in the third step. First, the specifier "high" is not specific enough. Second, the connection between situation C and action X is governed by probabilistic encounters, but the encounters that govern human behavior do not represent a strictly random process taking place repeatedly under constant conditions. Just as there may in principle be no law to the effect that *whenever* reason R occurs under certain conditions it will dominate all other reasons, so may there in principle be no law that *80 percent of the times* in which reason R occurs it will dominate.

The essential issue, then, is the issue of universality. Hempel in fact expresses doubt whether there are any universal principles such as those implied in the third step, but he does not categorically deny the possibility and goes on to grant it for the sake of the argument. It stands as one of the few suggestions in the philosophical literature about the actual content of a possible universal law of human behavior. Let us explore whether such third-step universals can exist by considering the primary social science implementation of this basic idea, namely, the rational choice model. To understand, predict, and explain behavior with the help of such models, one must either know or impute the relevant goals and beliefs of the individual, as well as the facts about key environmental conditions. Generally, the goals employed are straightforward self-interest goals. In this fashion, we get rational choice models of market behavior, voting behavior, sex-ratio behavior, war and international decision making, and so forth.

It is a critical question, however, whether the goals are indeed known or imputed. Which is it? It was clear to Hempel, as it must be to all of us, that "a situation of kind C" as specified in the first step of the syllogism must include a specification of the agent's relevant goals. From what source does this specification arise? The answer undoubtedly is that the goals are imputed by the investigator. This may best be seen, I suggest, in terms of Dennett's (1971) creative conceptualization of what he calls "intentional systems." (Many rational choice models predated Dennett's 1971 article by years—even centuries if we consider the classical treatises in economics—but his treatment may be seen as illuminating them in important ways. This section borrows much from Dennett's treatment.) The argument will be that use of imputed goals necessarily means nonuniversality and that it is not possible to formulate laws based on known or true goals. Furthermore, if the latter were indeed possible, there still could be no universal laws based on the principal of rationality.

When explaining or predicting the behavior of the person, group, computer, or other entity that one considers to be an intentional system, one predicts or explains from what Dennett calls the "intentional stance." There are alternatives. In particular, one could consider the entity to be a mechanism or formal system (my labels since Dennett does not supply one) and predict from the "design stance," that is, predict on the basis of knowledge of the working parts of the system and the program that runs it. Intentional systems as conceived by Dennett are not examples of a category found in nature but are rather creatures of human perception. One may go further and view the ontology as follows: all behaving systems have a design; therefore, there is no such thing in nature as an intentional system. For intentional systems, the *observer* considers the observed system to be a goal-seeking system, and the goals are imputed by the observer. Imputing goals is necessary because whatever they are, we have never been able to observe such a thing as a goal directly. We might ask a person, for example, what his or her goals are, and the person might tell us (although a dog or a computer as an intentional system could not do so on its own), but he or she cannot observe them directly either. We consider *ourselves* to be intentional systems and impute goals to *ourselves* on the basis of certain thoughts, feelings, and other evidence, but we are sometimes wrong and frequently are surprised to observe that our own behavior is simply not in conformity with what we thought were our goals.

(My own view, developed above, is not as extreme as Dennett's. Individual mammals, at least, do have goals if we consider a goal to be a certain affect-object dyad, and in principle these goals are observable. The fluid nature of the goals, however, and the current difficulty of observing them physiologically, make Dennett's model a reasonable one for the present discussion.)

In predicting from the design stance, the difference is not essentially that we know the goals but rather that no intellective goals or goal substitutes are needed. In predicting what a gum ball machine will do, for example, we do not base our claim on the knowledge that its goal is to give you a gum ball when you put a proper penny in but rather on the knowledge (even if a dim knowledge) that the penny will drop into certain slots and push certain levers, which will open certain doors and out will come the gum ball. For any such system, if we actually knew what "desires," "goals," and "reasons" were relevant, perhaps because we built the mechanism, those entities would not have to be "desires," "goals," or "reasons" but might rather become slots, circuits, loops, and levers. For systems viewed as what I have called mechanisms or formal systems, prediction and explanation are therefore deductive and empirical—deduced ultimately from the demonstrated laws of physics. For intentional systems, however, the basis is ultimately normative: given that the system is viewed as having this goal and that these are the circumstances, then the following is what it obviously *should* do and therefore what I predict it will do.

In a great many important cases, prediction from the intentional stance on the basis of imputed goals, when the design of the system is unknown, is nevertheless highly accurate. For this reason, rational choice models may be extremely powerful. It is in no sense my purpose here to argue that they are inferior to other social science approaches, none of which have any higher claim to universality. Impressive accuracy will obtain especially when the system has been adapted by one of two sources—people or evolution—to solve certain problems. The behavior for solving those problems in various circumstances may be quite evident and straightforward. Thus, if one explains and predicts behavior on the basis of the need to solve those known problems and on the known nature of the adaptation of the system, accuracy will be high indeed.

As just suggested, people can create mechanical and other systems to solve problems. It seems to be natural, indeed inescapable, for people to *think* (not the same as acting) rationally and intentionally. They are therefore capable of considering a certain state as "desired" and then of figuring out how to assign loops and levers so that the state in question will be attained in varying ways under varying conditions. Natural selection shapes organisms in the same ways. It gives them the equipment and the programs to solve the prevailing problems of their environments. Knowing the problems, the equipment, and the programs, it is fairly easy to do a good job of predicting accurately a great deal of behavior. In this light, other animals should be as fit subjects for rational choice models as people, and they are. We cannot help but talk about them as though they "wanted" certain things and are behaving in accord with a rational-normative program to obtain them. They should in fact be even better subjects for such models than people because they are simpler and their behavior is more obviously related to a manageable range of core problems. They are intentional systems because it is we, the observers, who define them as such, and they are "good" (well-functioning) intentional systems because evolution has adapted them admirably to solve a certain range of problems.

As I have noted, we see ourselves as intentional systems. I suggest that we do so in part (*a*) because we do not know the design of the mechanisms that produce our behavior (although we might use the intentional stance even if we did!), (*b*) because we—possibly unlike any other creature—happen to be specially equipped to view systems in that way, and (*c*) because whatever the design of the system that produces our intentional behavior, such as the affect-object system, it is likely to be complicated enough to make thinking about ourselves in those terms overly slow and cumbersome. The intentional system, in contrast, is wondrously parsimonious. On this last, Dennett notes that the designers of chess-playing computer programs presumably know the designs of their own programs and could conceivably predict moves on that basis as the program runs, but that is often far too complicated, and they will instead predict from the intentional stance: "It [the program] wants to gain control of the center (I know because I built it that way), so it will probably capture the bishop's pawn."

There are, however, limits to the validity of the intentional stance and limits, therefore, to the universality of models based on the principle of rationality. They are limited by such factors as the obscurity, multiplicity, fluidity, and complexity of the problems eligible for solution and the information that needs to be brought to bear. To take an extreme example, one might find it difficult to predict the behavior of an insane person with accuracy because that person is no longer programmed to solve the ordinary problems and, at the same time, has what we would consider to be distorted perceptions of the nature of the environment.

In rational choice models, there is no choice but to impute *simple* goals, otherwise the models would become swollen with ugly detail, and too much information would be necessary for prediction and explanation. Thus, rational choice models in economics impute simple goals of material gain, organizational models impute simple effectiveness goals, voting models are based on the closeness of each candidate's position to the voter's position, some war models depend heavily on the perceived probability of winning, and so forth.

In this light, it is to be expected that behavior must frequently be irrational, and therefore *not governed by a universal law* in the form of a rational choice model. Whenever systems behave in accord with considerations that are not imputed by the model, then under the model they behave irrationally. It is this that brings to light not only compulsive and neurotic behavior when viewed from the intentional stance but a good deal of everyday irrational behavior as well—that is, behavior that is much more common and seems more innocent (Hospers 1985), such as acting in terms of short-term benefit (e.g., telling off the boss) when long-term good clearly dictates the opposite. What, however, is the modeler's alternative? It is not possible to predict or explain human behavior accurately and universally on the rationality principle unless the "real goals" are considered. But how would the modeler find the "real goals" even if he or she were willing to throw parsimony to the winds and go for universality? One could ask the actors involved, but their answers would not be reliable. They do not always know their "real goals" themselves. One would have to look inside, physiologically, and do so repeatedly because the "real goals" may be constantly changing. And so we conclude that a theory based on the principle of rationality must either settle for the nonuniversality of simple intentional systems or become a variant of the affect-object paradigm. In that way, the ordinary rational choice model must fail in principle to serve as a universal law.

I suggest, moreover, that even if we tried to consider the affect-object paradigm itself to be a rational choice model, we would fail to fit it successfully into that category. At its foundations, and in a real and meaningful sense, human behavior is not rational (Lane et al. 1995). We can allow that peculiar *goals* such as misbegotten short-term interests are after all the person's goals and must therefore be accepted by the investigator as the premises upon which the rationality of behavior will be judged. However, rationality is not the fundamental basis for the selection of *means*—in fact, quite the contrary. The means-end procedure appears to grasp at means that have a pretty good probability of working but not necessarily at the most efficient means or in any other way the "best" means (cf. Lane et al. 1995). We often "don't think of" the best means, even if we have very recently used them. Further, we often choose some means over others just because they appeal to us (an affect tag at work somewhere), whereas the others are available and might well be more efficient and effective. There is room under the principle of rationality for odd choices of goals made because of the influence of affect, but there is not room for odd choices of means on the same basis. Rationality becomes meaningless if the definition is twisted to allow a less efficient and effective method to be used just because it happens to have greater emotional appeal. When means are selected on the basis of affect, as I hypothesize they frequently are, they become ends in themselves, and the idea of a rational model in that connection is destroyed. Any behavior may be selected at any time, depending on whether it appeals to us or not.

As a final note, we must recognize the logical possibility, no matter how far-fetched, that in some area of behavior, given the external circumstances, people will in fact always have the same goals by necessity and will always select the same optimal means of achieving them—again, not by the essentially temporary chance of common experience but by the necessity of common genetic structure. In that area, prediction and explanation by a universal principle would indeed be possible.

The behavior itself, however, would no longer be intentional; it should apparently concern our inquiry no more than, say, the phototropic behavior of a snail.

Biological Explanation

There is, however, a sense in which an animal phototropism should indeed be of interest to us: on the surface, our conclusions to this point do not make sense in the perspective of evolutionary biology.

A basic tenet of the sociobiologist is that, with very few exceptions, behaviors must be adaptive (i.e., advantageous to the individual as a result of the process of natural selection). The explanation is simple and, I think, incontrovertible. It is the same as the reason why nearly all traits of living organisms are adaptive. If a trait of individuals is not adaptive, then it is susceptible to being swamped in the population by a competing trait that *is* both adaptive and hereditary. In this perspective, the conclusion that there are no universal laws governing the generation of behavior must be wrong, or at least wrong-headed. True, there are genetic variations that produce variations in traits—including, presumably, behavioral traits. But there must also be widely shared gene complexes that produce behavior in common, behavior that has long been selected or that is now competing well in the struggle for selection. If many individuals of a species regularly find themselves in certain adverse circumstances, it is likely that the species will eventually respond with one certain behavior (sometimes a few competing behaviors). For example, when a predator is spotted, the Belding's ground squirrel will give an alarm call (and draw the predator's attention to itself) provided that it is surrounded by a great many relatives. But it is highly unlikely to sound the alarm when only very few of the other squirrels around it are related (Sherman 1977, cited in Trivers 1985: 110–14). And so must the case apparently be for numerous human behaviors. In short, it seems to me essential to grapple with the question of whether social scientists can develop explanations for at least some behaviors based in adaptation and the process and outcomes of natural selection.

If a behavior is commonly displayed but is not in place by virtue of having evolved through natural selection, then how is its occurrence to be explained? There would appear to be but two answers: the performance may either be random or be learned anew by each individual on the basis of experience. The widespread prevalence of random behavior is not credible. It implies far more self-neglecting and self-destructive behavior than is observed. Random behavior must regularly be defeated in evolution by the tendency toward self-interest.

It is over learned behavior that the issue is joined between proponents and opponents of sociobiological explanation. Opponents seem willing to allow that human and other animal behavior that is not controlled directly by genes (hunger drive, sex drive, etc.) is survival oriented, but it is so because it is culturally learned. To the sociobiologist, this position leaves too many unanswered questions. How can a species *avoid* the process of natural selection that will fix an advantageous behavioral trait? How is the ubiquity of self-interested behavior to be explained if there are no mechanisms whatever to give such behavior priority? It is not credible that each individual creature arrives at a self-interested pattern of behavior by its own learning process.

On the contrary, the natural starting position of the sociobiologist is that all behavior is hereditary and adaptive. If true, this position should perhaps lead social scientists and sociobiologists alike to develop an explanatory theory of each separate type of behavior (aggression, innovation, etc.) in terms of its adaptiveness in evolutionary time. For two reasons, however, this is not the path that has been followed in sociobiology. The response of scholars to these two issues has in fact led them to quite a different sort of behavioral theory (Wrangham 1980). Because the biological argument in favor of the fixation of behaviors through natural selection is compelling, it is potentially instructive for social science to explore the theoretical approach developed by this sister discipline.

The first reason is the existence and indeed the broad prevalence of altruism—behavior with a net benefit to another member of one's own species (excluding offspring) and a net cost to oneself. Altruism as just defined cannot possibly be both hereditary and viable. It would inevitably lose out to any more self-promoting genetic propensity that happened along. But altruism does commonly exist. If a behavior type that is so widespread is simply culturally learned and not genetic, then *this is a strong basis for the claim that any prevalent behavior might be learned.* The response to this challenge is that there actually is no altruism, except by occasional "mistakes." The discovery of the solution was made possible by the powerful concept of "inclusive fitness" introduced by Hamilton (1964). The inclusive fitness of an individual crea-

ture is the extent to which it leaves copies of its genes in future genera-
tions. The idea is crucial here because inclusive fitness is increased not
just by leaving offspring but by supporting relatives as well. Much
research subsequent to Hamilton's breakthrough has established that
most apparent altruism by far, particularly in nonhuman animals,
occurs between relatives. Thus, behavior such as endangering oneself
in the process of giving an alarm call does not have a net cost to the
individual because it turns out that warning calls mainly warn relatives. The enhanced probability of survival for all of the related individuals alerted is well worth the risk of one's own life in the coin of
inclusive fitness. In addition, Trivers (1971) has persuasively argued
that all remaining apparent altruism, except for occasional mistakes, is
reciprocal, and therefore (once again) not altruism at all: to the extent
that helping others exists, it leads to reciprocal helping with large
enough probability such that there is a net increase in inclusive fitness
for the "altruistic" individual.

What these two responses (relatives and reciprocation) suggest,
however, is that each individual sort of behavior, such as alarm calling,
is not controlled directly by its own dedicated genetic structure but
rather that there is some single, more generally applicable inherited
mechanism for deciding in individual instances whether an apparently
altruistic behavior will be inclusive fitness enhancing or not, so that on
that basis the behavior will sometimes be employed (e.g., when close
enough relatives are involved or when the expected value of reciprocation is high) and sometimes not. This is a strong step in the direction
away from the naive theory of direct genetic control of each individual
behavior. The question that would remain is only the nature of the general mechanism that enables correct decisions to be made on whether
or not to perform an altruistic behavior in a variety of circumstances.
We will return to that question in a moment.

The second reason why scholars have not adopted the separate-
mechanism theory concerns cultural complexity (Wrangham 1980).
There are so many different behaviors that there cannot possibly be
inherited genetic structures dedicated to each one, and the spread of
new behaviors within a population of animals is frequently so rapid
that the process of mutation and selection cannot possibly account for
it. Learning that is uninfluenced by the genes seems indicated, but this
violates the sociobiologist's conviction that such learning must
inevitably be swamped in evolutionary time by a hereditary propensity

toward a reliable, successful behavior. The paradox is plain. We may call it the fundamental dilemma of the biology of behavior: each behavior must be hereditary, but it is impossible that there be so many hereditary behaviors so rapidly fixed by selection. The solution must again be along the lines of a *general* genetic mechanism rather than a multitude of individual ones.

The general mechanism that has been widely accepted in response to these two issues is given in inclusive fitness maximization theory, articulated by Irons (1979), Durham (1979), and Alexander (1979). I will present and critique it briefly and then propose an alternative that I think may be more credible and that fortunately has more favorable implications for social research. In this way, I honor the basic argument in favor of biological explanation and credit the way in which it has been worked out in sociobiology up to a point. The reasons for departure beyond that point and the preferred alternative direction are outlined in the following paragraphs.

Inclusive fitness maximization theory hypothesizes only two evolved characteristics governing the choice of behaviors. The first is the propensity to estimate (not necessarily consciously, of course) the effects on inclusive fitness of the alternative behavioral possibilities that one faces, and the second is to choose the alternative that maximizes probable inclusive fitness. Thus, as Wrangham (1980: 174) puts it, "The frequency and distribution of behavioral traits are merely the result of a series of individual choices. However, the way choices are made depends on individual characteristics which are themselves biologically determined." Note that with the acceptance of this solution, the sociobiological approach no longer stimulates the development of an explanatory theory of each behavior in terms of its own adaptiveness. On the contrary, it would seem to impoverish explanatory theory and would at the same time obviate much of social research by providing the same explanation for all behavior, namely, that it is performed because in the circumstances it is "considered" by the individual creature concerned to maximize inclusive fitness. Wants and beliefs would seem to be minor. Environmental triggers should under this theory be far more important.

One must agree that the problems of altruism and cultural diversity imply the necessity of a general mechanism, but inclusive fitness maximization theory is a problematic candidate. My objections to this solution are the following. It is far-fetched to believe (*a*) that animals, and even humans, make probabilistic projections—even roughly or subconsciously—into the future specifying the various consequences of a behavior, each consequence bearing in some measure on inclusive fitness; (*b*) that animals are able to survey a collection of alternatives in this fashion and compare them, especially given the rapidity with which such decisions are generally made in the on-line, real-time world; and (*c*) that, with all the pitfalls of projection, estimation, and comparison as in (*a*) and (*b*), accuracy is nevertheless so great that behavior is as successful as it is, especially considering that individuals, even if their powers of calculation were high, could not possibly have enough information about the present and future to foretell with accuracy how various alternatives would work out in terms of inclusive fitness. Furthermore, (*d*) this theory does not account well for the making of "counterproductive" choices, especially by humans, such as the decision not to marry and not to have children: if we are programmed to maximize inclusive fitness, how can we deliberately perform acts that are so very unlikely to achieve that maximum?

As an alternative to inclusive fitness maximization theory for resolving the two issues militating against individual theories of behavior selection, I propose the affect-object paradigm. It serves at least as well to meet the challenges of altruism and cultural complexity, while avoiding the weaknesses of a biological system that depends on extraordinary perspicacity and myriad calculations. Happily, it also supports research in the social disciplines by justifying the common sort of explanation of human behavior we tend spontaneously to give—explaining by providing the operative reasons.

We need only see that the affect-object system—basically the same system that operates within us—evolved with the earliest mammals or even sooner and, with various species-specific changes, has been genetically copied and elaborated ever since. In the more complex species, it controls a very large proportion of all behavior. Individual behaviors are adaptive in this light only in the loose sense that the system as a whole that generates them is adaptive. The system is adaptive because, by parental teaching, group socialization, and direct experience with the environment, *affect tends overwhelmingly to become attached to objects in such a way as to guide behavior in self-protective, self-interested channels.* Parents teach offspring to avoid harm—essentially all harm—by virtue of the strong positive affect that is attached in all of us to the welfare of offspring, probably by direct genetic devices. I will come momentarily to the critical relationship between the individual and the social milieu, and how group socialization also functions to regulate behavior in the direction of net benefit to the individual.

The affect-object paradigm has much in common with the idea that behavior in general is learned by the individual rather than being inherited, so that a very broad and complex spectrum of behavior is permitted, except that in the perspective suggested here, both experience *and* biology (in the form of an inherited affect-object system) are critical. The weaknesses in inclusive fitness maximization theory are avoided in that there is no necessity for the calculation of probabilities or the projection of future effects. All is based on the association of objects with affect tags and with other objects by past experience (especially by socialization) and in some cases directly by inheritance. The paradigm allows for "mistakes," lots of them, and even for counterproductive choices. All that is necessary is that the system as a whole be adaptive relative to its alternatives. If a tendency toward maladaptive behavior should happen to creep into the genes, or if a certain behavior simply becomes very important in the survival equation, so that mistakes become extremely costly, specific adaptive behaviors can become established either (*a*) by genetic structures that control a particular behavior directly on the basis of environmental cues, as most behavior is controlled in less complex animals such as insects and fishes or (*b*), more likely, by genetically tying positive or negative affect to certain objects by natural selection—as in welfare of offspring or attraction to certain food sources—thus using the existing, general system to accomplish the end rather than cluttering up the chromosomes with controls for various behaviors under various conditions.

A highlight of the affect-object paradigm as a fundamental explanatory hypothesis in sociobiology is that it conveys the flexibility required to account for a certain amount of altruism in the context of a basic orientation toward self-interest.

As noted, a rigid or even fairly rigid altruism in the true sense of that term is impossible within the theory of natural selection. If altruistic acts have a cost in terms of inclusive fitness, this impossibility follows by definition because a loss of inclusive fitness means a reduction in progeny and the extinction of the genes for rigid altruism in competition with any less harmful ones. It is true that, in their important paper on this subject, Axelrod and Hamilton (1981) showed that cooperative behavior based on a particular strategy, once it is firmly established in a group, cannot be successfully "invaded" by egoism or self-ish behavior. This suggests a rigid altruism that contradicts the conclusion we just reached. The established cooperation they discuss, however, is not technically altruism. It is a *reciprocal* sort of helping behavior, one for which the payoff to each individual is actually higher than the payoff would have been for egoism. I believe that both Trivers (1971) and Axelrod and Hamilton (1981) are on thin ice to the extent that their hypotheses imply the need for the individual to distinguish between costly helping behavior that is likely to be reciprocated and true altruism, which is not. But it is important to see at any rate that in what we would be likely to call a highly cooperative milieu, individuals still do not run around constantly looking for ways to help others at a net cost to themselves. A very large number of potentially altruistic acts would in fact be regularly shunned in favor of more selfish behavior. I will suggest momentarily that it is primarily socialization by the subgroup that regulates the boundary between required altruism and permitted selfishness.

At the same time, a fairly rigid egoism is also not to be expected in a social mammalian species since the nature of the sociality itself will generally require a certain amount of altruism. What is important to note here is that it does not matter that many instances of helping behavior are not reciprocated on a one-to-one basis. If group norms (in any species) require a certain amount of such behavior—anything from grooming to birthday presents to hospital visits to potlatches—*it will usually be to the individual's advantage to conform,* for not doing so risks the loss of protection and other advantages that group membership in good standing confers. It is not at all necessary to be calculating in this regard, even subconsciously, or to be able to discern when helping behavior is likely to be reciprocated. It is only necessary to follow the pulls of the affect-object system because group socialization *means* the causation of affect tags and associations that will lead to cooperative behaviors in roughly adequate proportion. Much helping behavior must be considered truly altruistic in this perspective since it will be carried out without hope of one-to-one reciprocity. The advantages of group participation rarely depend on any one act. It is only the *pattern* of behavior that is "reciprocated," that is, that results in a net benefit to the individual relative to a much more egoistic orientation. True altruism, or performing more helping behavior than would be absolutely necessary, is then technically a "mistake," and probably one that most of us make, but not a mistake with such serious consequences that the basic mechanism that permits it is swamped by another in the process of natural selection. In this way, socialization adequately regulates egoism and altruism through the affect-object system. A rigid egoism, which is apparently all very well for bears and cheetahs given their ecological niches, will not do for social mammals such as horses, wild dogs, baboons, and humans. It would nullify the sociality that defines the species.

Last, there is one implication of this hypothesis connecting the affect-object paradigm with the sociobiology of behavior that underscores an important caveat long recognized in other perspectives. For each individual, intensive interaction with others cannot be spread evenly throughout a large population. Thus, there will be a tendency toward subgroups, and it is almost inevitable that socialization will result in much altruism within subgroups and much egoism between them.

In sum, even if the affect-object system turns out to generate wars that decimate this particular species in the long run, nothing beats it in our context all in all. With a few exceptions for survival-critical patterns, the biological argument should not lead us to study how certain *individual behaviors* become established as adaptive through natural selection. Rather, the affect-object system is the mechanism established by natural selection to produce intentional behavior that maximizes inclusive fitness. In this perspective, behaviors are *explained* by reasons and not by individual processes of natural selection. They are *caused* by operative reasons and not by specially dedicated gene complexes. The mechanism that works produces a staggering complexity and variety of human behavior out of minimal genetic variation, permitting both wide differences in behavior among cultures and subcultures and notable variety in responses to roughly similar situations even within them. At the same time, the number of seriously costly mistakes in altruistic and other behavior for the ordinary individual is tolerably low—lower than the number and seriousness of those expected under the likely competing mechanisms and low enough to keep this complex species, and indeed the whole biological class of mammals, reasonably competitive in the global struggle for existence.

References

Achen, Christopher H., and Duncan Snidal. 1989. Rational Deterrence Theory and Comparative Case Studies. *World Politics* 41 (2): 143–69.

Aggleton, John P., and Mortimer Mishkin. 1986. The Amygdala: Sensory Gateway to the Emotions. In Robert Plutchik and Henry Kellerman, eds., *Emotion: Theory, Research, and Experience.* Vol. 3, *Biological Foundations of Emotion.* New York: Academic Press.

Alexander, Richard D. 1979. Evolution and Culture. In Napoleon A. Chagnon and William Irons, eds., *Evolutionary Biology and Human Social Behavior.* North Scituate, MA: Duxbury Press.

Anscombe, G. E. M. 1957. *Intention.* Oxford, U.K.: Blackwell.

———. 1975. Causality and Determination. In Ernest Sosa, ed., *Causation and Conditionals.* London: Oxford University Press.

Arnold, Magda B. 1970. Perennial Problems in the Field of Emotion. In Magda B. Arnold, ed., *Feelings and Emotions.* New York: Academic Press.

Axelrod, Robert, and William D. Hamilton. 1981. The Evolution of Cooperation. *Science* 211: 1390–96.

Barley, Stephen R. 1990. The Alignment of Technology and Structure through Roles and Networks. *Administrative Science Quarterly* 35 (1): 61–103.

Beauchamp, Tom L., ed. 1974. *Philosophical Problems of Causation.* Encino, CA: Dickenson.

Becker, Marshall H. 1970. Sociometric Location and Innovativeness: Reformulation and Extension of the Diffusion Model. *American Sociological Review* 35: 267–82.

Berelson, Bernard, and G. A. Steiner. 1964. *Human Behavior: An Inventory of Scientific Findings.* New York: Harcourt, Brace & World.

Bower, Gordon H. 1981. Mood and Memory. *American Psychologist* 36 (2): 129–48.

Brand, Myles, ed. 1976. *The Nature of Causation.* Urbana: University of Illinois Press.

Campbell, Angus, Philip E. Converse, Warren E. Miller, and Donald E. Stokes. 1960. *The American Voter.* New York: John Wiley.

Campbell, Donald T., and Julian C. Stanley. 1966. *Experimental and Quasi-Experimental Designs for Research.* Chicago: Rand-McNally. Originally published as Experimental and Quasi-Experimental Designs for Research on Teaching. In N. L. Gage, *Handbook of Research on Teaching.* Chicago: Rand-McNally, 1963.

Child, John. 1972. Organizational Structure, Environment, and Performance: The Role of Strategic Choice. *Sociology* 6 (3): 1–22.

Collier, David. 1991. The Comparative Method: Two Decades of Change. In Dankwart A. Rustow and Kenneth Paul Erickson, eds., *Comparative Political Dynamics: Global Research Perspectives*. New York: HarperCollins.

Collingwood, R. G. 1940. *An Essay on Metaphysics*. Oxford, U.K.: Clarendon. Reprinted in part in Beauchamp, Tom L., ed. 1974.

———. 1946. *The Idea of History*. London: Oxford University Press.

Cronbach, Lee J. 1975. Beyond the Two Disciplines of Scientific Psychology. *American Psychologist* 30 (2): 116–27.

Davidson, Donald. 1980. *Essays on Actions and Events*. Oxford, U.K.: Clarendon Press.

Dennett, Daniel C. 1971. Intentional Systems. *Journal of Philosophy* 68 (4): 87–106.

Dienstbier, Richard A. 1984. The Role of Emotion in Moral Socialization. In Carroll E. Izard, Jerome Kagan, and Robert B. Zajonc, eds., *Emotions, Cognition, and Behavior*. Cambridge, U.K.: Cambridge University Press.

Dray, William. 1957. *Laws and Explanation in History*. Oxford, U.K.: Clarendon.

Duby, Georges. 1985. *William Marshal: The Flower of Chivalry*. Translated by Richard Howard. New York: Pantheon.

Ducasse, C. J. 1966. Critique of Hume's Conception of Causality. *Journal of Philosophy* 63 (6): 141–48. Reprinted in Beauchamp, ed.

Durham, William H. 1979. Toward a Coevolutionary Theory of Human Biology and Culture. In Napoleon A. Chagnon and William Irons, eds., *Evolutionary Biology and Human Social Behavior*. North Scituate, MA: Duxbury Press.

Eckstein, Harry. 1975. Case Study and Theory in Political Science. In Fred I. Greenstein and Nelson W. Polsby, eds., *Handbook of Political Science*, Vol. 1, *Political Science: Scope and Theory*. Reading, MA: Addison-Wesley.

Edwards, Patricia K., Alan C. Acock, and Robert L. Johnston. 1985. Nutrition Behavior Change: Outcomes of an Educational Approach. *Evaluation Review* 9 (4): 441–60.

Farrer, Austin. 1960. *The Freedom of the Will*. London: A & C Black.

Festinger, Leon. 1962. *A Theory of Cognitive Dissonance*. Stanford: Stanford University Press.

Freeman, Howard E., Robert E. Klein, John W. Townsend, and Aaron Lechtig. 1981. Nutrition and Cognitive Development among Rural Guatemalan Children. In Howard E. Freeman and Marion A. Solomon, eds., *Evaluation Studies Review Annual*. Vol. 6. Beverly Hills: Sage Publications.

Gallistel, C. R. 1980. *The Organization of Action: A New Synthesis*. Hillsdale, NJ: Lawrence Erlbaum Associates.

Gasking, Douglas. 1974. Causation and Recipes. *Mind* 64 (256): 479–87. Reprinted in Beauchamp, ed.

Geddes, Barbara. 1990. How the Cases You Choose Affect the Answers You Get: Selection Bias in Comparative Politics. *Political Analysis* 2: 131–50.

George, Alexander L., and Timothy J. McKeown. 1985. Case Studies and Theories of Organizational Decision Making. In Lee S. Sproull and Patrick D.

Larkey, eds., *Advances in Information Processing in Organizations.* Vol. 2 of Robert F. Coulam and Richard A. Smith, eds., *Research on Public Organizations.* Greenwich, CT: JAI Press.

Gergen, Kenneth J. 1973. Social Psychology as History. *Journal of Personality and Social Psychology* 26: 309–20.

German, Dwight C. 1982. Dopamine Neurons, Reward, and Behavior. *Behavioral and Brain Sciences* 5: 59–60.

Gilligan, Stephen G., and Gordon H. Bower. 1984. Cognitive Consequences of Emotional Arousal. In Carroll E. Izard, Jerome Kagan, and Robert B. Zajonc, eds., *Emotions, Cognition, and Behavior.* Cambridge, U.K.: Cambridge University Press.

Griffin, Donald R. 1984. *Animal Thinking.* Cambridge, MA: Harvard University Press.

Hamilton, William D. 1964. The Genetical Evolution of Social Behavior. *Journal of Theoretical Biology* 7: 1–52.

Hempel, Carl G. 1963. Reasons and Covering Laws in Historical Explanation. In Sidney Hook, ed., *Philosophy and History.* New York: New York University Press.

———. 1942. The Function of General Laws in History. *Journal of Philosophy* 39: 35–48.

Holland, Paul W. 1986. Statistics and Causal Inference. *Journal of the American Statistical Association* 81 (396): 945–60.

Hospers, John. 1985. Free Will and Psychoanalysis. In Joel Feinberg, ed., *Reason and Responsibility: Readings in Some Basic Problems of Philosophy.* 6th ed. Belmont, CA: Wordsworth.

Hovland, Carl I., Irwin L. Janis, and Harold H. Kelley. 1953. *Communication and Persuasion.* New Haven: Yale University Press.

Hull, Clark L. 1943. *Principles of Behavior: An Introduction to Behavior Theory.* New York: D. Appleton-Century.

Hume, David. 1955. *An Inquiry Concerning Human Understanding.* Edited by Charles W. Hendell. New York: Liberal Arts Press.

Hursh, S. R. 1980. Economic Concepts for the Analysis of Behavior. *Journal of the Experimental Analysis of Behavior* 34: 219–38.

Irons, William. 1979. Natural Selection, Adaptation, and Human Social Behavior. In Napoleon A. Chagnon and William Irons, eds., *Evolutionary Biology and Human Social Behavior.* North Scituate, MA: Duxbury Press.

Isen, Alice M., and Paula F. Levin. 1972. Effect of Feeling Good on Helping: Cookies and Kindness. *Journal of Personality and Social Psychology* 21 (3): 384–88.

Johnson, Patricia L. 1981. When Dying Is Better Than Living: Female Suicide among the Gainj of Papua New Guinea. *Ethnology* 20, no. 4 (October): 325–34.

Katz, Leonard D. 1987. *Bad Acts and Guilty Minds: Conundrums of the Criminal Law.* Chicago: University of Chicago Press.

————. 1982. Hedonic Arousal, Memory, and Motivation. *Behavioral and Brain Sciences* 5: 60.

Kim, Jaegwon. 1975. Causes and Counterfactuals. *Journal of Philosophy* 70: 570–72. Reprinted in Sosa, ed.

————. 1979. Causality, Identity, and Supervenience in the Mind-Body Problem. In Peter A. French, Theodore E. Uehling, Jr., and Howard K. Wettstein, eds., *Midwest Studies in Philosophy.* Vol. 4, *Studies in Metaphysics.* Minneapolis: University of Minnesota Press.

King, Gary, Robert O. Keohane, and Sidney Verba. 1994. *Designing Social Inquiry: Scientific Inference in Qualitative Research.* Princeton: Princeton University Press.

Kuhn, Thomas S. 1962. *The Structure of Scientific Revolutions.* Chicago: University of Chicago Press.

Lane, David, Franco Malerba, Robert Maxfield, and Luigi Orsenigo. 1995. Choice and Action. *Journal of Evolutionary Economics.*

Lang, Peter J. 1984. Cognition in Emotion: Concept and Action. In Carroll E. Izard, Jerome Kagan, and Robert B. Zajonc, eds., *Emotions, Cognition, and Behavior.* Cambridge, U.K.: Cambridge University Press.

Lee, Yoon-Shik. 1986. *The Child Restraint Requirement Law: An Impact Analysis and an Exploration of Program Evaluation Using Multiple Time Series.* Unpublished Ph.D. dissertation. Ann Arbor: University of Michigan, Department of Political Science.

Lewin, Kurt, Ronald Lippitt, and Robert K. White. 1939. Patterns of Aggressive Behavior in Experimentally Created "Social Climates." *Journal of Social Psychology* 10: 271–99.

Lewis, David. 1973. Causation. *Journal of Philosophy* 70: 556–67. Reprinted in Sosa, ed.

Lewis, Michael E., Mortimer Mishkin, Evgeni Bragin, Roger M. Brown, Candace B. Pert, and Agu Pert. 1981. Opiate Receptor Gradients in Monkey Cerebral Cortex: Correspondence with Sensory Processing Hierarchies. *Science* 211: 1166–69.

Liebman, Jeffrey. 1982. Understanding Neuroleptics: From "Anhedonia" to "Neuroleptothesia." *Behavioral and Brain Sciences* 5: 64–65.

Lijphart, Arend. 1971. Comparative Politics and the Comparative Method. *American Political Science Review* 65 (3): 682–93.

Lipset, Seymour M., Martin A. Trow, and James S. Coleman. 1956. *Union Democracy.* Glencoe, IL: Free Press.

Loeb, Louis E. 1974. Causal Theories and Causal Overdetermination. *Journal of Philosophy* 71: 525–44.

Mackie, J. L. 1965. Causes and Conditions. *American Philosophical Quarterly* 2 (4) October: 245–64.

————. 1980. *The Cement of the Universe: A Study of Causation.* Oxford, U.K.: Clarendon.

Malcolm, Norman. 1982. The Conceivability of Mechanism. In Watson, ed., *Free Will,* Oxford, U.K.: Oxford University Press.

March, James G. 1978. Bounded Rationality, Ambiguity, and the Engineering of Choice. *Bell Journal of Economics* 9 (2): 587–608.

Mayer, Arno J. 1967. Domestic Causes of the First World War. In Leonard Krieger and Fritz Stern, eds., *Responsibility of Power: Historical Essays in Honor of Hajo Holborn.* Garden City, NJ: Doubleday.

McKay, Harrison, Leonardo Sinisterra, Arlene McKay, Hernando Gomez, and Pascuala Lloreda. 1980. Improving Cognitive Ability in Chronically Deprived Children. In David Nachmias, ed., *The Practice of Policy Evaluation.* New York: St. Martin's Press.

Meiland, Jack W. 1970. *The Nature of Intention.* London: Methuen.

Michels, Robert. 1959. *Political Parties.* New York: Dover.

Mishkin, Mortimer, and Herbert L. Petri. 1984. Memories and Habits: Some Implications for the Analysis of Learning and Retention. In Larry R. Squire and Nelson Butters, eds., *Neuropsychology of Memory.* New York: Guilford Press.

———, and Tim Appenzeller. 1987. The Anatomy of Memory. *Scientific American* 256 (6): 80–89.

———, Barbara Malamut, and Jocelyne Bachevalier. 1984. Memories and Habits: Two Neural Systems. In Gary Lynch, James L. McGaugh, and Norman M. Weinberger, eds., *Neurobiology of Learning and Memory.* New York: Guilford Press.

Mohr, Lawrence B. 1982. *Explaining Organizational Behavior: The Limits and Possibilities of Theory and Research.* San Francisco: Jossey-Bass.

———. 1985. The Reliability of the Case Study As a Source of Information. In Lee S. Sproull and Patrick D. Larkey, eds., *Advances in Information Processing in Organizations.* Vol. 2 of Robert F. Coulam and Richard A. Smith, eds., *Research on Public Organizations.* Greenwich, CT: JAI Press.

———. 1995. *Impact Analysis for Program Evaluation.* Second edition. Thousand Oaks, CA: Sage.

Molnar, George. 1969. Kneale's Argument Revisited. *Philosophical Review* 78 (1): 79–89. Reprinted in Beauchamp, ed.

Monod, Jacques. 1971. *Chance and Necessity.* New York: Alfred Knopf.

Mueller, Jonathan. 1984. Neuroanatomic Correlates of Emotion. In Lydia Temoshok, Craig Van Dyke, and Leonard S. Zegans, eds., *Emotions in Health and Illness: Theoretical and Research Foundations.* New York: Grune and Stratton.

Panksepp, Jaak. 1982. The Pleasure in Brain Substrates of Foraging. *Behavioral and Brain Sciences* 5: 71–72.

Perrow, Charles. 1963. Goals and Power Structures: A Historical Case Study. In Eliot Freidson, ed., *The Hospital in Modern Society.* New York: Free Press.

Rech, Richard H. 1982. Neurolepsis: Anhedonia or Blunting of Emotional Reactivity? *Behavioral and Brain Sciences* 5: 72–73.

Roethlisberger, F. J., and W. J. Dickson. 1939. *Management and the Worker.* Cambridge, MA: Harvard University Press.

Rogers, Everett M., with F. Floyd Shoemaker. 1971. *Communication of Innovations.* New York: Free Press.

Roitblat, H. L. 1982. The Meaning of Representation in Animal Memory. *Behavioral and Brain Sciences* 5 (3): 353–406.

Schachter, Stanley. 1959. *The Psychology of Affiliation*. Stanford: Stanford University Press.

———. 1970. The Interaction of Cognitive and Physiological Determinants of Emotional States. In Leonard Berkowitz, ed., *Advances in Experimental Social Psychology*. Vol. 1. Stanford: Stanford University Press.

Scheier, Michael F., and Charles S. Carver. 1982. Cognition, Affect, and Self-Regulation. In Margaret S. Clark and Susan T. Fiske, eds., *Affect and Cognition*. Hillsdale, NJ: Erlbaum.

Scriven, Michael. 1959. Truisms As the Grounds for Historical Explanations. In Patrick Gardiner, ed., *Theories of History*. Glencoe, IL: Free Press.

———. 1966. Causes, Connections and Conditions in History. In William Dray, ed., *Philosophical Analysis and History*. New York: Harper and Row.

———. 1976. Maximizing the Power of Causal Investigations: The Modus Operandi Method. In Gene V. Glass, ed., *Evaluation Studies Review Annual*. Vol. 1. Beverly Hills: Sage Publications.

Selltiz, Claire, Lawrence S. Wrightsman, and Stuart W. Cook. 1976. *Research Methods in Social Relations*, 3d ed. New York: Holt, Rinehart, and Winston.

Sherif, Muzafer. 1936. *The Psychology of Social Norms*. New York: Harper.

———, and Carolyn Sherif. 1953. *Groups in Harmony and Tension*. New York: Harper.

Sherman, Paul W. 1977. Nepotism and the Evolution of Alarm Calls. *Science* 197: 1246–53.

Simon, Herbert A. 1967. Motivational and Emotional Controls of Cognition. *Psychological Review* 74: 29–39.

———. 1977. The Logic of Heuristic Decision Making. In *Models of Discovery*. Dordrecht: Reidel.

———, Allen Newell, and J. C. Shaw. 1979. The Process of Creative Thinking. In Herbert A. Simon, ed., *Models of Thought*. New Haven: Yale University Press.

Sinnamon, Harry M. 1982. The Reward-Effort Model: An Economic Framework for Examining the Mechanism of Neuroleptic Action. *Behavioral and Brain Sciences* 5: 73–75.

Skinner, B. F. 1953. *Science and Human Behavior*. New York: Macmillan.

———. 1964. Behaviorism at Fifty. In T. W. Wann, ed., *Behaviorism and Phenomenology*. Chicago: University of Chicago Press.

Skocpol, Theda, and Margaret Somers. 1980. The Uses of Comparative History in Macrosocial Inquiry. *Comparative Studies in Society and History* 22 (2): 174–97.

Smiley, Marion. 1991. *Moral Responsibility and the Boundaries of Community: Power and Accountability from a Pragmatic Point of View*. Princeton: Princeton University Press.

Smith, M. Brewster. 1976. Social Psychology, Science, and History: So *What*? In

Melvin Manis, ed., Social Psychology and History: A Symposium, *Personality and Social Psychology Bulletin* 2: 438–44.

Sosa, Ernest, ed. 1975. *Causation and Conditionals*. London: Oxford University Press.

Spiegler, B. J., and Mortimer Mishkin. 1981. Evidence for the Sequential Participation of Inferior Temporal Cortex and Amygdala in the Acquisition of Stimulus Reward Associations. *Behavioural Brain Research* 3: 303–17.

Staats, Arthur W. 1975. *Social Behaviorism*. Chicago: Dorsey Press.

Stinchcombe, Arthur L. 1990. *Information and Organizations*. Berkeley: University of California Press.

Strawson, P. F. 1985. Causation and Explanation. In Bruce Vermazen and Merrill B. Hintikka, eds., *Essays on Davidson: Actions and Events*. Oxford, U.K.: Clarendon.

Suppes, Patrick. 1984. *Probabilistic Metaphysics*. Oxford, U.K.: Basil Blackwell.

Tomkins, Silvan S. 1981. The Quest for Primary Motives: Biography and Autobiography of an Idea. *Journal of Personality and Social Psychology* 41 (2): 306–29.

Trivers, Robert L. 1971. The Evolution of Reciprocal Altruism. *Quarterly Review of Biology* 46: 35–57.

———. 1985. *Social Evolution*. Menlo Park, CA: Benjamin/Cummings.

Von Wright, Georg H. 1971. *Explanation and Understanding*. Ithaca, NY: Cornell University Press.

Warnke, Georgia. 1984. Translator's introduction to Karl-Otto Apel, *Understanding and Explanation: A Transcendental-Pragmatic Perspective*. Cambridge, MA: MIT Press.

Watson, Gary, ed. 1982. *Free Will*. Oxford, U.K.: Oxford University Press.

Watson, John. B. 1930. *Behaviorism*. New York: W. W. Norton.

Wise, Roy A. 1982. Neuroleptics and Operant Behavior: The Anhedonia Hypothesis. *Behavioral and Brain Sciences* 5: 39–53.

Wrangham, Richard W. 1980. Sociobiology: Modification with Dissent. *Biological Journal of the Linnean Society* 13: 171–77.

Zajonc, Robert B. 1980. Feeling and Thinking: Preferences Need No Inferences. *American Psychologist* 35 (2): 151–75.

———, and Hazel Markus. 1984. Affect and Cognition: The Hard Interface. In Carroll E. Izard, Jerome Kagan, and Robert B. Zajonc, eds., *Emotions, Cognition, and Behavior*. Cambridge, U.K.: Cambridge University Press.

Index

Behavior (*continued*)
control of, 2
distinct from action, 59
generalizations in quantitative
research, 145–46
independent, 59–60
laws governing, 50–52
limbic system in regulation of,
80–81
possibility of laws covering, 2
predicting, 84–86
pure, 59–60
reason does not demand, 63–64
reasons for, 5
relation of reason and decisions to,
65, 93–95
relation to affect-object paradigm,
78–83
role of encounters in, 134
selected by means-end procedure,
7
in sociobiology, 158–59
Behavior, human
covering-law model of, 151–52
hypothetical probabilistic law of,
138
no laws governing, 7–8, 134–35
physical causation of intentional,
135
probabilistic, 8
Behavior, intentional
defined, 59, 88
dependent on probabilistic
encounter, 24
physical causation of, 116, 142
physiological mechanism of, 2–3
produced by affect-object system,
91–92
wants that may determine, 68–
69
See also Means-end procedure
Behavior, rational, 86–88
Behaviorism
as alternative to affect-object paradigm, 84–86
explanation of behavior in, 84

in light of affect-object paradigm,
84–85
Belief
in affect-object system, 87
as component of reason, 58
representation in affect-object system, 87
Berelson, Bernard, 148
Bower, Gordon, H., 72, 73, 81, 83
Brain structures, 80–81
Brand, Myles, 41, 42

Campbell, Angus, 146
Campbell, Donald T., 107
Carver, Charles S., 75, 82
Case studies
bases of support for potential internal validity of, 113–15
criticism of, 117
to establish causal relations in
social research, 9
as research design, 113
small-n research design within,
9–10
in social research, 108–15
Causal chains
counterfactual, 31–32, 34
factual, 27, 91–92
function of encounters in factual,
27
with preliminary encounters, 132
in production of behavior, 133–34
Causality
circularity criterion challenge to
counterfactual definition, 23
collateral effects challenge to counterfactual definition, 20–22,
36–38
counterfactual definition, 14–16, 38
Hume's definition and analysis, 13,
16, 42–43
make- and let-happen challenge to
counterfactual definition, 22–23,
29, 38
modified counterfactual definition,
15–16, 27–40

Physical science
  differences from social science,
    135–37
  similarities to social science, 137
Physiological system, 71
Possibility, significant, 144–45
Predictions
  from intentional stance, 154–56
  in physical and social sciences,
    135
Preference, 88
Priority setting, 82–83
Probability sampling, 110

Quantitative findings (as singular
    explanations), 145
Quantitative research, 99

Randomness, 139
Rational choice model, 152–53,
    156–57
Rationality
  in affect-object paradigm, 86–88
  in behavior, 151–58
  in selection of means, 157
Reasoning, causal
  basis for factual, 98–99
  as basis for quantitative research,
    99
  complementary, 122–23
  factual, 98–102, 106, 117–29
  function of factual, 100
  physical, 102–6, 116–29
  physical causes in small-n study,
    125
  in social science, 98
Reasoning, quantitative, 120
Reasons
  for behavior, 5
  cause behavior under certain con-
    ditions, 66–68
  as causes, 49–50, 58, 63–67, 88, 134
  conscious, 95–96
  desire and belief components of, 58
  explain actions, 60–61
  nonconscious, 70–83

occurrence in affect-object system,
    134
occurrence with other reasons, 89
in rational-psychological realm, 87
relation to behavior, 63–65
relation to decisions and behavior,
    93–95
thoughts in form of, 58, 61
Reasons, operative
  as causes, 86–93
  internal actions among related
    entities, 92
  as physical causes, 92
  as physical causes of behavior,
    92–93, 116
  relation to intentional behavior, 58
Reasons, true
  defined, 70
  as factual causes, 91–92
Redundancy
  in counter-factual definition of
    causality, 17–20
  in factual causal reasoning,
    100–101
Regularity
  independence of and association
    with causation, 56
  link between physical causation
    and, 49
Regularity theory of causation
  of Hume, 4, 42–43, 48
  problems with Hume's idea of,
    47–56
Relations
  between behaviors and their expla-
    nations, 8
  causal relations in probabilistic
    encounters, 8
  as laws, 138
Replication, 110–12
Research
  distinction between theoretical and
    applied, 149–50
  explanatory, 144–45
  generalizations in quantitative,
    145–46

DATE DUE